894751

DATE DUE

D1413803

Queen Victoria

BY E. F. Benson

AN ILLUSTRATED
BIOGRAPHY

CHATTO & WINDUS
LONDON

Published in 1987 by Chatto & Windus Ltd
30 Bedford Square, London WC1B 3RP

First published in Great Britain by Longmans, Green and Co.
Ltd 1935. This illustrated abridged edition first published in
Great Britain by Chatto & Windus Ltd 1987

British Library Cataloguing in Publication Data
Benson, E. F.
Queen Victoria.
1. Victoria, *Queen of Great Britain*
2. Great Britain—Kings and rulers—Biography
I. Title
941.081′092′4   DA554
ISBN 0 7011 3267 1

Designed by Christos Kondeatis

Picture research by Philippa Lewis

Abridged by Deborah Singmaster

Typeset by Rowland Phototypesetting Ltd
Bury St Edmunds, Suffolk

Printed in Great Britain by Butler & Tanner Ltd
Frome, Somerset

ACKNOWLEDGEMENTS
The following illustrations are reproduced by gracious permission of Her Majesty the Queen: 29;
(from the Royal Archives, Windsor) 6, 53, 78, 85, 91, 92, 118, 125, 139; (from the Royal Library,
Windsor) 13, 22, 45, 58, 60 (bottom), 77, 83, 90, 94, 119. BBC Hulton Picture Library: 8, 44, 48, 51,
69, 96, 113, 114, 116, 129, 135, 136, 138, 143, 146, 151. The Bodleian Library, Oxford: 108, 147.
Bridgeman Art Library: (R. L. Bayne-Powell Collection) title page, 95. Christie's, London: 15.
Fotomas Index: 21, 36 (top), 28, 56, 74, 98, 117, 155. Mansell Collection: 7, 9, 18, 20, 26, 35, 37,
39, 41, 62, 70, 71, 82, 88, 106, 120–1, 123, 131, 148. National Portrait Gallery, London: 16, 76,
109. Royal Commission on the Ancient and Historical Monuments of Scotland: 60 (top). Victoria
and Albert Museum (photos Eileen Tweedy): 19, 31, 47, 89, 100, 101, 128, 158, 160 (Museum
Photo), 64, 65. Weidenfeld & Nicolson Archives: 10, 33, 36 (bottom).

Colour illustrations between pp 40 and 41. BBC Hulton Picture Library: 5 (top left); Bridgeman Art
Library: 1, 2, 4, (Wolverhampton Art Gallery) 5 (top right and bottom) 6 (top), 8. Her Majesty the
Queen: 3, 6 (bottom) 7 (both). Colour illustrations between pp 104 and 105. Bridgeman Art
Library: (Forbes Magazine Collection) 5, 6, 8. Fotomas Index: 1. Mansell Collection: 7 (both). Her
Majesty the Queen: 2, 3, 4.

Contents

The Duchess of Kent with the infant Princess Victoria
clutching a miniature of her dead father.

Princess Victoria aged 10, heir to the throne. After a
drawing by R. T. LANE.

I · HEIR TO THE THRONE

WHEN QUEEN CHARLOTTE, wife of George III had given birth to no less than fifteen Princes and Princesses she may well have thought that the Royal House of Hanover would not lack heirs to the throne of England for many generations to come. But when she died in the year 1818 its stability was by no means assured, for though twelve of her children were still alive they were all getting on in years, and she had not a single grandchild, male or female, who could ever wear the Crown or defend the Faith. Grandchildren there were in plenty, for her third son William, Duke of Clarence, had no less than ten olive-branches round about his table at Bushey, but as all of these were the offspring of the charming actress Mrs. Jordan they were of no avail for dynastic purposes. A similar dynastic defect afflicted the two children of the Queen's sixth son Augustus, Duke of Sussex, for their mother was Lady Augusta Murray, daughter of the Earl of Dunmore, and the Royal Marriage Act debarred them too from the throne. There had once been a direct heir of the third generation, Princess Charlotte, daughter and only child of George, Prince of Wales. In 1816 she had married Prince Leopold of

Saxe-Coburg, but she had died in November 1817 in giving birth to a still-born seven-months' boy. Thus in 1818 though twelve brothers and sisters might, if they died in order of strict seniority, sit in turn, one after the other, on the throne of their fathers, there were none to succeed them. Valhalla would be denuded of its gods.

The vigorous matrimonial measures taken over the next year were swiftly rewarded, for whereas in 1818 there had been no heir of the third

George III and Queen Charlotte on the terrace at
Windsor, preceded by their numerous children, 1781.

generation to the English Crown, there were born, during 1819, no less than four. The Duchess of Clarence in March gave birth to a daughter, and though the baby only lived a few hours, there were now grounds for hope on the part of its parents and for cruel apprehension on the part of its uncles, that more might follow. In May the celebrated German midwife Frau Siebold was in attendance at Kensington Palace, whither the Duke and Duchess of Kent had returned from Amorbach, in order that their expected child should be born on English soil, and on May 24 the Duchess was safely delivered of a daughter, who at the moment of her birth was the direct inheritor of the throne. The Duchess of Cambridge, out in Hanover, gave birth to a son, christened George, and by way of an unexpected bonus with regard to heirs, the Duchess of Cumberland, who had now been married for four years, became the mother of a son, who was also named George. These two Georges, being offspring of younger brothers of the Duke of Kent did not get in the way of his baby daughter: she, by right of her father's primogeniture, came first, Prince George of Cumberland second, and Prince George of Cambridge third. Three small infants, of almost identical age, one at Kensington Palace, one at Kew

Engraving of Queen Victoria's father, the Duke of Kent,
who died in 1820 shortly after her birth.

and one at Hanover were sleeping and squawling and being fed each in happy ignorance of the chances that governed the prodigious destiny of one of them. But the stability of the House of Hanover had in the briefest of possible periods been buttressed and amazingly re-inforced, and the uneasy spirit of Queen Charlotte must have been reassured.

Within months after the birth of his daughter, Alexandrina Victoria, the Duke of Kent died and his widow moved with her household into Kensington Palace. There were herself, her daughter Feodore, now in her thirteenth year and the baby of eight months, and the principal members of her household were her lady-in-waiting Baroness de Späth, her daughter's governess Fräulein Louise Lehzen, as, as secretary and Con-

Cartoon of 1819 depicting the Dukes of Clarence,
Cambridge, Kent and Cumberland in the race to
produce an heir.

troller of her Household, her late husband's equerry and executor, Sir
John Conroy. He had a wife, and several children, the youngest of whom
was a baby daughter Victoire, who became Princess Victoria's constant
playmate.

When Victoria was six years old, the King, George IV, invited her to
Windsor for the first time. This visit was a wonderful experience for the
small girl, and nearly fifty years later she recorded it in a paper of
reminiscences of her childhood. The party went over to Royal Lodge,
and in spite of his gout and his huge obesity and his wig (wigs in
combination with aprons had caused Princess Victoria to regard Bishops
with intense horror), she found him a very dignified and charming
person. "Give me your little paw," he said to her: and then in turn he
gave her a miniature of himself set in diamonds, which was an Order to
be worn by Princesses on the left shoulder, and Lady Conyngham pinned
it on for her. His kiss, as she remembered in later years was rather

dreadful, for his face was covered with grease-paint. Next day, the same family party from Kensington, driving to Virginia Water, where the King had been embellishing the beauties of nature, met him in his phaeton going there with the Duchess of Gloucester. He stopped and said "Pop her in," and there Victoria sat between him and Aunt Gloucester. Her mother was "much frightened," but Victoria was delighted, and they drove to the Fishing Temple where was a large barge, and they all embarked on it and fished. Another barge followed them with a band on board which made music for the anglers. The King paid particular attention to-day to Princess Feodore who was a very lovely girl: satirical people said that perhaps he would marry her. Then came tea with peaches in a cottage by the lake, after dinner the party again went to Royal Lodge, and there was more music in the Conservatory which was lit up by coloured lamps. At the end of one piece the King told his niece to choose the next tune, and she chose "God Save the King." Altogether she made a very good impression on "Uncle King," and he asked her down to Windsor again next year, and shewed a certain interest in the household at Kensington Palace by creating Fräulein Lehzen a Baroness of his kingdom of Hanover.

By this time, the education of Princess Victoria had become almost intensive. It was an age in which young ladies in England were assiduous in accomplishments, and it was only right that the Princess should excel them all. They must be able to sit down and play the piano of an evening, or to stand up and sing. Everyone sang: even King George sang, and when Maestro Rossini, the great operatic composer came to England, he was sent for to Windsor, and sang duets with the Sovereign. And young ladies must be equally ready to dance with grace and modesty and they must be able to sketch in water-colours and draw with pencil. "Touches" were taught: there was an oak-tree touch, and a beech-tree touch and a birch-touch, so that from these significant handlings of the pencil their friends would be able to identify the species of the vegetable. Languages were also a necessary equipment: German and French must spring to adolescent lips. With German the small Princess had no difficulty, for she was surrounded by natives of that nationality, but when it came to learning English her German accent must be eliminated. So Mr. Sale, the organist at St Margaret's, Westminster, taught her singing and playing, and Mr. Westall R. A. taught her drawing, and Mlle. Bourdin taught her to dance the minuet, and M. Grandineau to acquire the true French accent, and Mr. Steward of Westminster School taught her English grammar (which she never really mastered), and arithmetic. This troupe of specialists, who came daily to Kensington Palace, were under the supervision of a general Minister of Education, the Reverend George Davys. He had begun his instruction when Victoria was only four years old, and as the girl grew formed a very high estimate of her abilities.

But a greater responsibility rested on the new Hanoverian Baroness than on any of these, for she was "personal attendant" on the Princess, and it was her task to correct not merely faults in her compositions but faults in her character. But truth and a sense of honour were admirable foundations, and they were certainly as firmly laid in Victoria's character as her quick temper, and Lehzen, perceiving that the little girl was extremely affectionate and would do anything for those she was fond of, set out to make herself loved, and, for disciplinary purposes, feared. "I adored, though I was greatly in awe of her," was her pupil's statement of her childish relations with the Baroness. For her mother she felt less adoration and certainly more fear. Years afterwards on her mother's death she found, with pangs of bitterest remorse, the diary which revealed to her for the first time how truly devoted and tender was the Duchess's love for her, for she had never suspected it. She referred in later years to her "sad and lonely childhood," but it would appear to have been much the same as that of any other little girl of the upper classes, who was being very carefully brought up by a lonely mother, and who had the misfortune (though in this case there was a bright lining to that) of not having any brothers. One inmate of the Palace, Sir John Conroy, the Controller of the Household and her mother's confidential secretary, she detested.

In 1832 the Duchess started making autumn progresses through the kingdom with her daughter accompanied by the inevitable Sir John Conroy: in itself the idea was admirable, for they stayed at inns or at big country-houses such as Chatsworth or Holkham or Burghley, and the Princess got to see the country and the homes of her future subjects.

The Princess was thirteen when these tours began, and her mother told her she must now begin to keep a Journal in a book she gave her for that purpose, describing what she saw and did, and the journal begun in 1832 was continued till her death nearly seventy years later. Up till her accession these entries were evidently made with the knowledge that her mother would cast a critical eye over them. Many entries were jotted down first in pencil, no doubt *en route*, and we may imagine Lehzen

Victoria's drawing of her governess, Baroness Lehzen,
who supervised every detail of her life and education.

reading them over and perhaps suggesting omissions or amplifications before they were inked in to be shewn Mamma. The first day of this tour was merely travel and we read:

"We left K. P. (Kensington Palace) at 6 minutes past 7. The road and scenery beautiful. 20 minutes past 9. We have just changed horses at Barnet, a very pretty little town . . . The country is very bleak and chalky. 12 minutes to 12. We have just changed horses at Brickhill. The country is very beautiful about here . . . At ½ past 5 we arrived at Meriton: and we are now going to dress for dinner. ½ past eight. I am undressing to go to bed. Mamma is not well and is lying on the sofa in the next room. I was asleep in a minute in my own little bed which travels always with me."

Her tastes began to develop, and with them enthusiasms expressed with a profusion of italics and capital letters. This was in emulation of Uncle Leopold who freely employed these aids to emphasis, and Victoria adopted it for good. Dancing was one of these enthusiasms, music was another, and many were the Saturday evenings, after the tour was over, when she was taken to the opera, where a ballet was always a part of the programme. There grew an enthusiasm for animals, ponies and dogs in especial, but never cats. There was "sweet little Rosy" (or Rosa) her pony, and "dear sweet little Dash," a King Charles spaniel given to her mother by Sir John Conroy; twice in one day Victoria dressed up this unfortunate animal "in a scarlet jacket and blue trousers."

Then came the greatest treat yet, for in commemoration of her coming sixteenth birthday the Duchess gave a superlative concert at Kensington Palace with all the stars of Opera singing: Grisi, Rubini, Malibran and Lablache. On the day itself her "present-table" was loaded with gifts: Dashy gave her an ivory basket full of barley-sugar and chocolate, and, in addition to the concert, her mother gave her an enamel bracelet containing a lock of her hair, and Feodore another, also with hair, and Sir John Conroy a writing case, and Mr Hatchard the bookseller a prayer-book: there were so many that she forgot, except in post-script, to mention the sapphire and diamond earrings from the King and Queen. But the best of all the presents was the concert, and for almost the only time in the Journal the Duchess became "*dear* Mamma." The day was Sunday, and Dean Davys preached a very appropriate sermon (Joshua 24, 15). Sixteen seemed a great age, and gave rise to most edifying reflections and resolutions: "I feel that the two years to come till I attain my 18th birthday are the most important of any almost. I now only begin to appreciate my lessons, and hope from this time on to make great progress."

The same summer (1835) the Princess was confirmed, and we get a glimpse of that very sincere, very uncomplicated sense of religion which remained her steadfast and unfailing guide throughout her life. "I felt deeply repentant for all that I had done which was wrong and trusted in God Almighty to strengthen my heart and mind; and to forsake all that is bad and follow all that is virtuous and right." That "foi de charbonnier"

The 16-year old Victoria, with her dog Dash, painted by
GEORGE HAYTER.

was always hers: she never took the slightest interest in dogmas and ecclesiastical rites and theological minutiae, and the old lady of nearly eighty who considered M. Comte's views "so very extraordinary," and thought no more about such stuff, was exactly the same simple and uncritical Christian as the girl of sixteen had been. Three days afterwards she received her first Communion, and up till the day of her death she would have endorsed what she wrote in her Journal then: "It is a very

King William IV, whose short reign from 1830–37
preceded Victoria's.

solemn and impressive ceremony, and when one recollects and thinks that we take it in remembrance of the death of our blessed Saviour, one *ought*, nay *must* feel deeply impressed with holy and pious feelings!" After that day she received the Sacrament twice every year, spending the whole day, if possible, in quiet seclusion. Neither ecstasy nor doubt ever troubled her: the one was as incomprehensible to her as the other.

In 1836 Victoria's Uncle Leopold, King of the Belgians, arranged for his nephews Ernest and Albert to visit England. Leopold had long intended that Prince Albert, younger son of Duke Ernest of Saxe-Coburg and Princess Louise of Saxe-Gotha-Altenburg, should marry his niece. Victoria at once settled that she loved these cousins *"much more dearly* than any other cousins in the *world*." Albert was the handsomest, and, though not seventeen, was as tall as his brother: both were clever, but he was the cleverer and the most "reflecting": both drew beautifully but he the more beautifully, and both were "*very very* merry and gay and happy, like young people ought to be," but Albert's wit and fun was the most unfailing.

Nothing marred the delight of those three weeks while "i miei carissimi cugini" were at Kensington, and very bitter were Victoria's tears when they left. Uncle Ernest took with him a note from his niece to Uncle Leopold, which showed how warmly she embraced the destiny which she already knew he had shaped for her:

"I must thank you, my beloved Uncle, for the prospect of *great* happiness you have contributed to give me in the person of dear Albert. Allow me then, my dearest Uncle, to tell you how delighted I am with him in every way. He possesses every quality that could be desired to make me perfectly happy. He has besides the most pleasing and delightful exterior you can possibly see. I have only now to beg you, my dearest Uncle, to take care of the health of one now so *dear* to me, and to take him under *your special* protection. I hope and trust that all will go on prosperously and well on this subject of so much importance to me." . . . Laus Deo!

Albert, it is to be feared, had not found the visit so charged with rapture as his prospective bride. He missed his tutor, Herr Florschütz, so he wrote to his step-mother, the climate made him bilious, and these late hours, one, two and even four in the morning made it a frightful struggle to keep awake. His quarters at Kensington Palace were comfortable but cramped, and of his hostess and her daughter all he said was that "Aunt Kent was very kind, and our cousin also is very amiable." In fact Victoria seemed to have made no impression whatever on him, and her superlatives contrast rather discouragingly with his indifference.

King William IV was seriously ill when Victoria came of age on May 24 1837 and Uncle Leopold sent his friend and adviser Baron Stockmar over to England to advise her in the event of the King's death.

Princess Victoria wrote: "Stockmar has *been* and *is* of the *greatest* possible use, and be assured, dearest Uncle, that he possesses *my most entire confidence*."

Queen Victoria with her mother, the Duchess of Kent, at
the Chapel Royal, Windsor.

Popular print of 'Victoria I, Queen of England', 1837.

II · ACCESSION

THE KING DIED very early on the morning of June 20, and that night Victoria recorded the most momentous event of her eighteen years: "I was awoke at 6 o'clock by Mamma, who told me that the Archbishop of Canterbury and Lord Conyngham were here and wished to see me. I got out of bed and went into my sitting-room (only in my dressing-gown) and *alone*, and saw them. Lord Conyngham (the Lord Chamberlain) then acquainted me that my poor Uncle, the King, was no more, and consequently that I am *Queen*."

The interview was quite short, and then the Queen of England went to her room and dressed, then breakfasted while Stockmar talked to her. At nine came Lord Melbourne, "whom I saw in my room, and of COURSE *quite* ALONE as I shall *always* do all my Ministers." She held her first Council: Lord Melbourne and her Uncles Cumberland and Sussex conducted her, but she went in quite alone and was not at all nervous. She gave audiences to four Officers of State "all in my room and alone," and had a second interview with Stockmar. She dined alone: there is a story, perhaps not authentic, that her mother sent to tell her that dinner was

Contemporary engraving of the proclamation of Queen
Victoria's accession at St James's Palace.

ready and that she was waiting. Her messenger returned with a scribbled
line, "The Queen will dine alone." A third interview with Stockmar
followed, and "a very important and a very *comfortable* conversation"
with Lord Melbourne. There was a fourth interview with Stockmar and
she said goodnight to her mother, and for the first time in her life she slept
alone in her own room.

From six o'clock that morning she had taken up her tremendous
destiny with the complete certainty that she was perfectly capable of
fulfilling it. She was Queen, so she entirely believed, by the Will of God:
nobody else was Sovereign of England, and that constant repetition of
the word "alone" in her account of this first day of her reign testified to
her appreciation of that no less than to the end of her mother's domestic
domination.

Her character was already completely formed, and though for the

Celebrations at Brighton, on Victoria's first visit as
Queen, 4 October 1837.

twenty-one years of her coming married life, she was rapturously content
to surrender herself wholly to the guidance of her husband, it was not
altered thereby. The loneliness of her early childhood, the domination of
her mother to which she had silently and lovelessly submitted, had driven
her into herself and generated, in the very core of her nature, a vein of
iron. She was full of spontaneous gaiety, she was capable of eager and
intense enjoyment, she was warmly affectionate, but she had also this
inflexible will which caused her, when once she had come to a conclusion, to be rigidly tenacious of it, and these conclusions were the easier to
arrive at because she had not and never would have the slightest touch of
intellectual subtlety. Her mind was that of a supremely honest and
capable young woman, with an unfailing supply of the most robust
common sense and a total absence of distinction: on to this were grafted
the instincts of a Queen. It was an uncomplicated make-up, but likely to

21

Victoria's sketch of Lord Melbourne with her terrier,
Islay.

be highly efficient, the more so because it was not handicapped by fine perceptions: and it consisted of untiring industry, white hot conscientiousness, great good sense, but little sensitiveness, delight in her duties, self-reliance and an unquestioning belief in God.

She plunged into Sovereignty: she received addresses from the Houses of Parliament: she held a Levée at which three thousand people kissed her hand: she gave audience to Foreign Ambassadors: she chose her Household (or rather Lord Melbourne chose it for her): she prorogued Parliament: she read despatches that arrived from her Dominion of Canada: her Sister the Empress of Russia sent her the Order of St Catherine. From the first her Prime Minister won her entire trust and she made up her mind about him at once. "He is indeed a most truly honest, straightforward and noble-minded man, and I esteem myself most fortunate to have such a man at the head of the Government: a man in whom I can safely place confidence. There are not many like him in this world of deceit." He pleased her no less personally, and she registered: "He is my *friend*, and I know it."

There is something extraordinarily attractive in this self-portrait which so unwittingly she gives of herself in her letters and Journals. Nothing came amiss to this small plain girl, with her ready laughter and her vivacity and her frolic welcome to all these new experiences, with her bubbling affection and withal her regal dignity when occasion required. It was the greatest fun being Queen of England, and she recorded that this summer of 1837 was "the *pleasantest summer* I have ever passed in my life." Her first big public appearance to her people was when "*in all my finery*" she attended the Lord Mayor's banquet in the great State carriage drawn by eight of the famous "cream-coloured" horses. George I had brought that equine strain along with his mistresses from Hanover, and George IV when he went there for his second coronation had replenished the stock. They were scarcely carriage-horses; they were half *percherons*, and their cart-horse blood admirably served the stately foot-pace progress of that ponderous fairy-story wain with its glass sides, and its gilded crowns and tritons. It took two hours to get from Buckingham Palace to the Guildhall, and the tremendous reception that the girl met with brought home to her more vividly and intimately than ever what it meant to be Queen. Civic ceremonies followed, she knighted the Sheriffs among whom was a Jew, Mr. Moses Montefiore. Never before in English history had a Jew received the knighthood: the Queen thought this quite right, and the precedent was made. Then came dinner which lasted well over two hours, and she returned home not in state, but in a landau with a pair of horses and no guard, a young girl with a bad headache, passing through the thronged streets, Queen of her people. She hoped there had been no accidents in those vast crowds: "I cannot say," she wrote in her Journal, "HOW gratified, and HOW *touched* I am by the very brilliant, affectionate, cordial, enthusiastic and *unanimous* reception I met with in this the *greatest* metropolis in the *World* . . . I feel *deeply grateful* for this display of affection and unfeigned loyalty and *attachment* from my good people. It is much more than I deserve, and I shall do my utmost to render myself worthy of all this love and affection" . . .

The man who was to do most to help her in this endeavour was her Prime Minister, Lord Melbourne. From the first interview the Queen had with him on the day of her Accession she had put herself into his hands in the conduct of all business relating to the State, but Uncle Leopold who had approved, indeed ordered that, could not have foreseen the personal friendship which so speedily ripened between this elderly man, approaching sixty, and the girl of eighteen. Lord Melbourne had had considerable experience in his life of sunny weather and of stormy, and it had wrought in him a kindly but slightly cynical indifference to weather of every kind, so that he realized that all is vanity, but that some vanities were far more interesting than others. He had great charm, great attraction for women, and his simple and sincere affection for this young girl who almost immediately found in him her third father (Uncle Leopold being "il mio secondo padre") was shot with a romantic chivalry for the "little Queen" on whom such destinies rested and who gazed at the vast prospect with such blue-eyed, open-mouthed appreciation.

He had thought it "a damned bore" when in 1834 King William had sent for him to form a Ministry: he was not sure whether he would take office or not, but now the most brilliant company at Holland House which hung on his words and wit, was less to his mind than the eager chatter of this girl, which she recorded with such gusto in her Journal. He saw her daily over the affairs of her realm, and she listened to his advice with utter confidence in his wisdom, but their intercourse was by no means over when business was finished. They rode together; he dined with her, whether at Windsor or Buckingham Palace, practically every night, always sitting on her left.

Sometimes he seems not to have been in a very amiable humour and flatly disagreed with all she said. She did not resent this: she was learning. And if, as occasionally happened, Lord Melbourne fell asleep in the middle of one of these dialogues, instead of being offended she was only afraid that he was not quite well. Another day she was a few minutes late in returning from her ride, and found that Lord Melbourne who was coming to see her had gone home. She only blamed herself for not being punctual.

Sometimes their conversations resembled nothing so much as the topics introduced to a patient by a psycho-analyst (Lord Melbourne being the patient), and we must figure the Queen as asking him an interminable series of questions, for no one could talk, of his own accord, with such staggering irrelevance. His mind was probed in every direction, Eton Montem, Lord Duncannon's teeth, the over-rated quality of bird-song, the inebriate habits of his servants, the dullness of gardens, the inordinate amount of pastry Lord Melbourne used to eat when a boy, the difficulty of breaking cannibals of their habits because they thought nothing was so good as human flesh, Islay's (her dog) passion for licking his spectacles. Every topic under the sun was discussed, and every day she wrote down all he had said.

Between balls and political crises and rides, and the eager discharge of her duties, and preparations for the Coronation in June, the spring of 1838 was a full time. When Uncle Leopold had been at Windsor last summer, the Queen had hoped that he and Aunt Louise would come to it, but representations had been made that Kings and Queens (though uncles and aunts) were not wanted, and he took the hint.

There was a private rehearsal for the Queen in the Abbey on the day before the ceremony, which was fortunate, for the two thrones on which she would sit before and after the Crowning were too low, and had to be raised. On the morning of June 28, she was awakened at four o'clock by

the roar of the guns in the Park. There was a tremendous welcome for her
as she drove to the Abbey in the State coach: she was ineffably proud "to
be the Queen of *such* a *Nation*," and hoped that none of her people
would be "crushed or squeezed." With an amazing minuteness she
described in her Journal every movement in the pageant: the changes of
her robes, the placing of the Crown on her head and the simultaneous
assumption of their coronets by all the peers and peeresses, the Enthro-
nization, the Homage, the various unforeseen effects like Lord Rolle (as
if playing a charade on his own name) rolling down the steps to the
throne, how she was given the Orb before the right moment, how the
Archbishop insisted on putting the ruby ring on her wrong finger – the
clergy would have been the better for more rehearsals – and it hurt
terribly to get it off again, and how *loaded* she felt with the Crown on her
head and the Orb in her left hand and the Sceptre in her right! But what
most went to her intimate heart was the "fatherly" look Lord Melbourne
gave her when she was crowned, and the smile she exchanged with her
dear Lehzen. Nimble indeed had Lehzen and Späth been on that day: they
had seen her leave Buckingham Palace and arrive at the Abbey: they had
seen her leave the Abbey and were back at Buckingham Palace to see her
return. It was eight hours since she had left at ten that morning, but she
was not feeling tired, and Lord Melbourne dined. "And you did it so
well: excellent!" said he, with the tears in his eyes. After dinner they had
their usual talk: he had had breakfast in the Jerusalem Chamber before
the ceremony: whenever "clergy or a Dean and Chapter had anything to
do with anything, there's sure to be plenty to eat." And she stayed up till
midnight looking at the fireworks and illuminations in the Green Park.
Not till forty-nine years later did she again go to the Abbey as the central
figure of a great pageant, and that was to celebrate the fiftieth anniversary
of her accession. There was no State coach then, nor Royal robes nor Orb
nor Crown nor Sceptre, and once more she was alone in her long
widowhood, as she had been to-day in her girlhood, and a little old lady
in a black satin dress, with a cavalcade of Princes, sons and sons-in-law
and grandsons, for escort on the drive, came up the nave, leaning on her
stick, to give thanks to God for His loving mercies to her. She was tired
then, but once more after dinner she admired the illuminations.

Romantic engraving of Victoria in her coronation robes.
After a painting by A. E. CHALON.

Popular lithograph showing Victoria's proposal to Albert.

One of Victoria's favourite images of Albert, mezzotint
after a painting by R. THORBURN.

III · ALBERT

THE KING OF THE BELGIANS and Queen Louise, not having come to the Coronation, paid the Queen a visit in September at Windsor. It must have been painfully clear to him how completely Lord Melbourne had supplanted him as adviser in all things pertaining to the State and how he had encroached on her affection. But he hoped to make good this loss, for Albert's terms at the University of Bonn were over, and Baron Stockmar was going to act as tutor-cicerone to him in Italy. Stockmar was Leopold's second self as regards Albert and Albert's future and the forming of his nature, and thus Leopold hoped to get back on the swings what he had lost on the roundabouts.

But he had not sufficiently allowed for the change that had taken place in his niece since Albert's visit in 1836, when she had accepted Uncle Leopold's choice for her with such warmth of welcome. In those lonely and restricted years at Kensington Palace all those Coburg cousins had seemed to her tall and handsome and talented and delightful, but now she was Queen of England, revelling in her dignities and powers, and that made a difference to her valuations. The thought of her marriage was a burden on her mind, and in the spring of 1839 she introduced it into her conversation with Lord Melbourne.

Now for the first time Albert's name was mentioned between them: hitherto they had only discussed her marriage in the abstract. Lord Melbourne did not like it. "Cousins," he said, "are not very good things, and those Coburgs are not popular abroad: the Russians hate them." Instantly she whisked round, "By all that I heard," she said, "Albert would be just the person . . ." Besides who else was there? She thought it was quite out of the question that she should marry a subject. She could not see why she should marry for three or four years yet. "I said I dreaded the thought of marrying: that I was so accustomed to have my own way that I thought it was 10 to 1 that I shouldn't agree with anybody."

All these conversations betokened a disquieted mind. She was just at the age when adolescence makes private hells of its own, and she had no girl friend nor an older woman in whom she could confide. She had quite determined to have no intimacy with the Ladies of her Household, Lehzen the middle-aged spinster would be of no use in such a difficulty and the woman to whom a girl naturally goes in these perplexities common to her age, her mother, was the very last person to whom she would dream of taking her troubles. An unhappy spring.

When Uncle Leopold proposed that Albert and Ernest should visit in 1839 she sent him a sort of ultimatum on this "odious" subject: "Even if I should like Albert," she wrote, "I can make *no final promise this year*, for at the *very earliest* any such event could not take place till *two or three years hence*. For independent of my youth and my *great* repugnance to change my present position, there is *no anxiety* evinced *in this country* for such an event." And, if she found that she liked him "as a friend, and as a *cousin* and as a *brother* but not more," she intended to refuse him without being guilty of any breach of promise since she had never given any.

When the cousins arrived at Windsor after a frightful crossing from Antwerp, the Queen thought them "grown and changed and embellished," and Albert, she saw with emotion, was "*beautiful*." It was an immense compliment to be told by her Ladies that he was like her, and Lord Melbourne when appealed to said he saw the resemblance at once.

Prince Albert and his brother Ernest, in historical costume, 1851. Engraving after painting by R. THORBURN.

And he danced so well (it was permissible for her to valse and galop with him), and for three days they rode together and looked at drawings and played games of Tactics and Fox and Geese, and proximity did its perfect work. Besides, as she told Lord Melbourne, he was so amiable and good-natured, whereas her own temper was so bad, and she revoked the opinion she had expressed to him before that a man's looks did not matter, and owned that beauty was an advantage. Next day her mind was made up, and she told Melbourne she would marry him in a year's time. But he read her intention better than that, and when he suggested that the wedding should be celebrated much sooner, she agreed, and the two, taking Albert's consent for granted, instantly went into Committee, as to what should be "done" for him. He must be made a Field Marshal, she thought, and a Royal Highness but not a Peer: Parliament would see about provision for him. She would have to propose to him herself, for, as she told Aunt Gloucester afterwards, Albert "would never have presumed to take such a liberty as to propose to the Queen of England."

Next day she sent for him and told him "it would make me *too happy* if he would consent to what I wished," and they were betrothed. She said she was quite unworthy of him, she felt it was a great sacrifice on his part, and the date was to be early in February . . . Then the chief contriver, Uncle Leopold, must be informed. Albert was *perfection*, she wrote; she loved him more than she could say: she was bewildered by her happiness.

And what of the chosen bridegroom? His letters to his relatives and friends were those of a man whose emotions were absolutely untouched by the decision that had given his future bride such rapture, but who met the situation with pluck, clearly realizing the opportunities it would afford him of doing good. "Life has its thorns," he wrote to his stepmother, "in every position, and the consciousness of having used one's powers and endeavours for an object so great as that of promoting the good of so many, will surely be sufficient to support me." To his friend and tutor Stockmar he wrote: "The event has come upon us by surprise, sooner than we expected . . . I will not let my courage fail. With firm resolution and true zeal on my part, I cannot fail to continue noble, manly and princely in all things."

As for Victoria, we must suppose that she was so much in love with him that she did not see or did not care that quiet affection rather than responsive rapture was all he could give her. Indeed the usual rôles of bride and bridegroom were reversed, she was the passionate wooer of her consenting mate.

The cousins stopped at Windsor for a month, and then Albert returned to the beloved Coburg which he must so soon leave for ever, while the Queen plunged into all the official preliminaries to the marriage which

Queen Victoria rides the political see-saw on the back of John Bull. Wellington, representing the Tories, is out of favour, while Melbourne, for the Whigs, is in the ascendant. Cartoon of 1838.

was now fixed for February 10, 1840. There was plenty to occupy her and abundant opportunity for the vein of iron.

From Coburg Albert wrote to the Queen about the important question of his Household. He was under the impression that he would have a say in the matter. "I should wish particularly that the selection should be made without regard to politics: for if I am really to keep myself free from all parties, my people must not belong exclusively to one side. It is very necessary that they should be chosen from both sides – the same number of Whigs as Tories . . . I know you will agree in my views." But here he was disappointed: she told him it would not do, and he might rely on her to choose proper people for him. Again he wanted a German as his private secretary. Quite impossible: his Secretary must be English. In fact she had chosen him already, Mr George Anson, who at present was Lord Melbourne's Secretary. That would not, as Albert thought, look like political partisanship, for Mr Anson had never been in Parliament. She was Queen, she knew what was right, and she chose his entire Household for him without his seeing any of them. Once more he wrote to her suggesting that the honeymoon at Windsor might be extended beyond the two or three days allotted to it. But no: "You have not at all understood the matter. You forget, my dearest Love, that I am the Sovereign, and that business can stop and wait for nothing . . . therefore two or three days is already a long time to be absent (from London) . . . This is also my own wish in every way." Later, her views about the necessity of her being in London while Parliament was sitting were considerably modified.

But now it was time for Albert to make the great sacrifice. The Queen sent out an Embassy to Gotha for his investiture with the Garter, and after due festivities, Duke Ernest with his two sons set out for England in the Royal carriages despatched by the Queen for their conveyance. She had decided that the wedding should not take place at Westminster Abbey, for that would be like another Coronation, but at the Chapel Royal, St James's. Then there was her mother: the Queen suggested that, as she would not drive to the wedding in full state, her mother should go with her. The very fact that she did not take that for granted shows perhaps how wide was their alienation.

Albert and his father and brother arrived on February 8, two days before the marriage. On the wedding morning the Queen sent to his bedroom in Buckingham Palace a little folded note without envelope:

"Dearest – How are you to-day, and have you slept well? I have rested very well and feel very comfortable to-day. What weather! I believe, however, the rain will cease.

Send one word when you, my most dearly loved bridegroom, will be ready.

Thy ever-faithful,
Victoria R."

He was ready: he had been ready since October when he had decided to accept her devotion and to make the best use of the opportunities it afforded him to increase the happiness and welfare of England's millions.

After the marriage service there was a very formal banquet at Buckingham Palace, and the Queen bade adieu to her old life. She took off her white satin wedding gown, with its deep flounce of Honiton lace, made

The Queen in her wedding dress. After a drawing by
W. DRUMMOND.

after an old design, and her diamond necklace and ear-rings, and put on a white silk gown trimmed with swansdown, and a white bonnet under the eaves of which nestled a sprig of orange blossoms. Then there was just time for ten minutes' talk alone with Lord Melbourne, and, with her invariable accuracy, she noted the hour "20 m to 4 till 10 m to 4." She praised his well-fitting coat – that was an old joke between them – and told him he must be down at Windsor two days hence in time for dinner. Did he guess then that his reign was over and another begun? He said "God bless you, ma'am," and Albert came to fetch her, and they said goodbye to her mother and drove off to Windsor alone a few minutes before 4 o'clock.

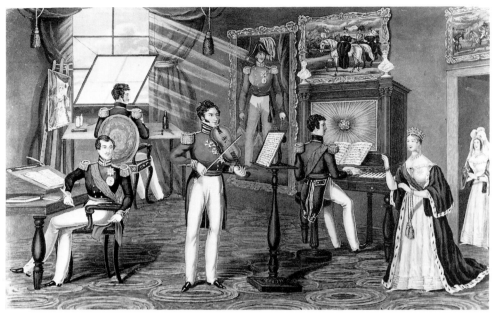

Cultural Life at Windsor. Albert writing; Ferdinand of
Portugal etching; Leopold, King of the Belgians on the
violin; Ernest at the keyboard, 1844.

The closely observed birth of the Queen's first child,
Princess Victoria, in 1840.

The Prince of Wales and the Princess Royal, Victoria's
two eldest children.

IV · DOMESTIC FELICITY

T HE DAY AFTER HER MARRIAGE, the Queen wrote to Uncle Leopold from Windsor:

"I do not think it *possible* for anyone in the world to be *happier* or AS happy as I am. He is an Angel . . ." From that considered opinion she never wavered. But still she was the Queen of England: two days of honeymoon she allowed herself, and then the whole Court followed the bridal pair down to Windsor. They danced after dinner that night and the next (for some reason this was considered rather indelicate): then back they went to London, and Albert began to learn what it meant to have married the Queen of England.

In those intervening months he had thought it all out, and he meant, cautiously and gradually, so that her jealousy of her Sovereign rights should not be aroused, to make himself indispensable to her not only as an adored husband, but as her sole counsellor. He meant to permeate her, to sink his directing individuality in her, to put his will, his perceptions, his ability so much at her service as to be fused with her own.

The acquiring of political influence, which from the first was part of the

Prince's programme of "promoting the good of so many," was a matter that had to be gone about cautiously, for, as the Queen had warned him, the English would strongly resent any sort of direct interference on his part in politics, and it was only through building up in her a conviction of his wisdom and discretion that he could hope to establish himself. She was very jealous of her position as Sovereign: she and her Ministers and they alone were directors of the Realm. Physically she adored him, she rightly appreciated the nobility of his character, and her protective tenderness of the Angel who had left all for her sake was a valuable asset to him, which he did not neglect. When, a fortnight after his marriage, his father, Duke Ernest, with his suite in floods of tears at leaving the beloved young Prince in England, went back to Coburg, he told Victoria that she "had never known a father, and could not therefore feel what he did." Brother Ernest, however, remained on for a couple of months, and their parting in May was even more desolating. They sang "Abschied" together, and when Ernest had gone, all that Albert, left alone with his bride, could say was "Such things are hard to bear." Her heart was wrung for him. "Oh! how I did feel for my dearest precious husband at this moment," she wrote in her Journal. "Father, brother, friends, country – all he has left and all for me. God grant I may be the happy person, the *most* happy person, to make this dearest, blessed being happy and contented! What is in my power to make him happy, I will do."

Albert recognised that this was a propitious moment to advance a step. She knew he was lonely, and he reproached her for not treating him with confidence either on "trivial matters," or on anything connected with politics. This disturbed her, and she consulted Lord Melbourne, acknowledging that it was wrong of her not to do so; she said it was indolent of her but she preferred to talk to him on subjects other than these. Melbourne urged her to be more open with him on political matters; he was anxious "that the Queen should tell and shew him everything connected with public affairs." She took this excellent advice, and before the marriage was six months old, he was supplied by Melbourne with Foreign Office despatches, and occasionally, by the Queen's special invitation, he was present at her interviews with her Ministers. That was a great step. As for the "trivial matters," these no doubt referred to the running of the establishments at Buckingham Palace and Windsor, for, as Albert wrote to his friend Prince William of Lowenstein, he was not the master of his house but only the husband of its mistress. But indeed the Queen was scarcely mistress there herself: the control of the staff and the stable and the kitchens was in the charge of various officers of State, and the only way to get anything done was through Baroness Lehzen. She would have to go, but the time had not come for that, and meantime the

A 'scrap' showing Victoria reading a speech from the throne, flanked by the supportive Albert.

Prince noted the million signs of a ludicrous extravagance that yielded the minimum of comfort, and he instructed Stockmar to do a little quiet investigation into the domestic economy of Palaces and embody his discoveries in a memorandum.

Socially, the Prince was not making a very good impression. He was shy, he was ill at ease among these aliens, and he cloaked his shyness with a stiff and frigid dignity. He lacked the light touch which gives effervescence to social intercourse, and women could hardly fail to feel his punctilious unconsciousness of their charms. Uncle Leopold had thought that when he was sixteen he was getting "an English look," but at twenty he had certainly grown out of it. Nor did his tastes show any trace of

Anglicization, he was steadfast to that unfortunate resolve of his to remain a true German. He was not unathletic, he rode well, and while a student at Bonn had won a fencing competition, but he thought of all sports, shooting and hunting and the like, merely as salubrious diversions and did not understand, nor could he, the English mania for taking them seriously and spending whole days in the saddle or the coverts. On the other hand he regarded as high and ennobling objects, worthy of a man's serious study, pursuits which the barbarous English considered only as pretty diversions for a woman. It was nice for women to record in their sketchbooks the beauties of nature, to stand up and sing after dinner or removing rings and bracelets to sit down and play. But Albert wooed the Muses with reverent ardour; he was never happier than when improvising on his new organ at Buckingham Palace; he encouraged the Queen in her singing and sang himself with her. These duets were not private diversions only: they gave a concert at the Palace, conducted by Signor Michele Costa, and the Royal pair sang "Non funesta crudele" by Ricci, and the Queen sang the trio "Dunque il mio bene" from Mozart's "Magic Flute" with Rubini and Lablache, the most admired tenor and bass of the Italian opera and they both took part in choruses by Haydn and Mendelssohn. In emulation of this melodious evening Lady Normanby, the Mistress of the Robes, gave another musical party in which amateurs sang with professionals. On this occasion the Prince was not singing, and overcome by his usual evening somnolence, he had a quiet sleep, sitting next to his hostess and looking beautiful.

Then he had greatly cordialized the relations between the Queen and her mother, and before long that reconciliation warmed into love. He was a peace-maker, and among his tactful operations was a tranquillising of his wife's impulsive and violent temper: Uncle Leopold had exercised just such a control over Princess Charlotte before either of them was born. The Queen adored him: he was daily getting more perfect in her eyes, and his deep seriousness of purpose, his conscientiousness, his industry, and, above all, his untarnishable respectability were just what was needed to obliterate from the mind of the nation the Hanoverian misconception of monarchy. Perhaps, for all his oddities, his pedantry, he might prove to be exactly the man for the moment.

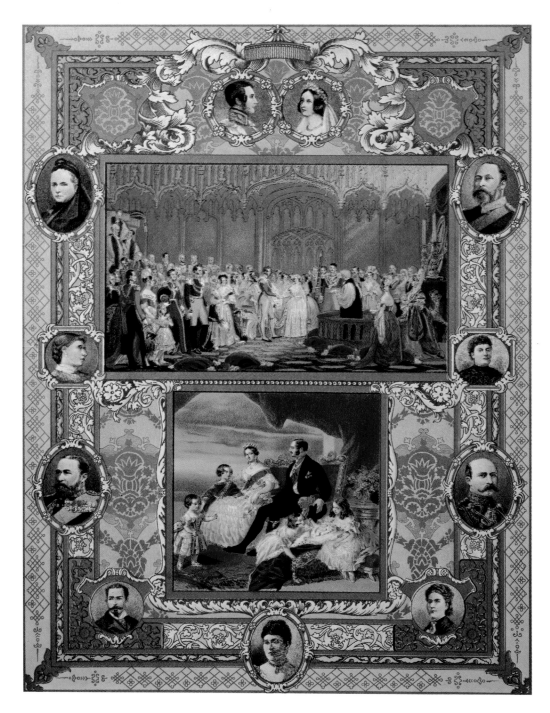

Colour print commemorating Queen Victoria's Jubilee,
including vignettes of her wedding and a family group.

Queen Victoria at the opera.
Oil painting after E. T. Parris.
Prince Albert in evening dress with the garter star.
Miniature by Robert Thorburn.

Queen Victoria riding in Windsor Home Park. Painting
by SIR EDWIN LANDSEER.

Popular colour prints: The Royal Family at Windsor
Castle, by EDWARD WELLS, 1850. Victoria and Albert
dancing together. Victoria and Albert travelling in the
royal train with King Louis-Philippe of France, by
E. PINGRET, 1844.

Views of Osborne and Windsor.
Windsor, Christmas 1850, presents around the tree.
Watercolour by J. ROBERTS.

The arrival of Victoria and Albert at a ball in the Hôtel de
Ville, during their visit to Paris in 1855.
Watercolour of a ghillies ball at Balmoral in 1859.

Victoria in a carriage with her mother, the Duchess of
Kent; Sir Robert Peel, Wellington and Prince Albert
mounted. Painting by HENRY BARRAUD, 1845.

In June an adventitious circumstance suddenly caused a recrudescence of loyalty. The two were driving out one evening up Constitution Hill, meaning to pay a call on the Duchess of Kent in Belgrave Square, when a crazy young fellow, called Edward Oxford, fired two pistol shots at them from the distance of five or six yards. They both behaved with the most unassumed coolness, and after the man had been seized, drove on to the Duchess's house so that she should not be alarmed by any chance report

Assassination attempt in 1840, by Edward Oxford, on
Constitution Hill.

that might reach her. After that they went on for their drive in the Park to show the public (as Albert characteristically wrote to his grandmother) "that we had not, on account of what had happened, lost all confidence in them." Though he sincerely despised popularity, nothing could have been more popular than such simple pluck, and at Opera and racecourse they were hailed with universal enthusiasm.

The Queen's first child was born on November 21, 1840, and Ministers of the Crown, the Archbishop of Canterbury and the Bishop of London were in a room outside the open door of the bedchamber to be witnesses to the authentic existence of a new-born baby. Then Dr Locock's voice was heard from within, a little disappointed, but appreciative of the rank of the august pilgrim. "Oh, Madam!" he said, "it is a Princess": and a voice from the bed replied, "Well, next time it will be a Prince." During the mother's swift convalescence, Albert, she wrote in her Journal, looked after her as if he had been her mother. He was very busy, for by special and rather peremptory order, the Queen directed that the despatch-boxes from the Foreign Office, which had been withheld for a day or two after the birth, until she could attend to affairs of State again, should be sent to him. She rather demurred to Uncle Leopold's hope that this daughter would be the first of many children, and wrote to him that he could not really wish her to be "Mamma *d'une nombreuse famille*, for I think you will see with me the *great* inconvenience a *large* family would be to us all, and particularly the country, independent of the hardship and inconvenience to myself." Doubtless, as regards the country, she was thinking what an intolerable expense her uncles had been to it, but all these objections soon ceased to weigh with her.

The Court went to Windsor for Christmas, and the Queen, who previously had far preferred the gaiety and bustle of London, began to feel differently about the country, and it was with great reluctance that she came back to town at the end of January. The reason was not far to seek: Albert hated late hours and the dense air of London, and he felt in Paradise on the hill above the Thames. "Now I am free: now I can breathe," he used to exclaim, and he and the Queen would take Eos his greyhound out for a walk before they settled down to work, and in the afternoon he was busy out of doors with the new pleasure ground he was laying out below the terrace and the building of the new stables.

But in spite of this high domestic felicity, there was political trouble brewing over the question of Protection. In this summer of 1841 the Whig Government was tottering, and the Queen was threatened with losing Lord Melbourne. But now the prospect was not so desolate, for Albert was with her and she resolved to face it quietly and philosophically.

At the ensuing Elections a large Tory majority was returned, and in August the Whigs resigned, and the Queen asked Sir Robert Peel to form a Government. It was bitter to lose Lord Melbourne: for over four years she had seen him almost daily, and during that period only once had as many as eleven days elapsed without her having a talk with him. In his last interview he had spoken to her in the highest terms of Prince Albert's judgment and discretion, and, since he himself was leaving her, she could not do better than to seek the Prince's inestimable advice on all political matters, and confidently rely on his judgment.

Melbourne did his utmost to smooth Peel's way for him, and establish friendly relations between the Queen and the new Ministry. She thought for instance, when they came to kiss hands, that they looked "cross." He assured her that they were only shy and embarrassed, and that Peel was most anxious to work harmoniously with her.

On November 9, 1841, almost exactly a year after the birth of her first child, the Queen was transacting business till after ten o'clock in the morning, but then hurried messages were despatched to the great Officers of State to come at once to Buckingham Palace for that barbarous ritual of waiting in the next room for the labour to be done, and before eleven struck a male heir to the English throne was born, even as the mother had prophesied less than a year ago, that the next child would be a Prince. "A wonderfully strong and large child," she wrote to Uncle Leopold, "with very large dark blue eyes, a finely formed but somewhat large nose, and a pretty little mouth: I *hope* and *pray* he may be like his dearest Papa. He is to be called Albert, and Edward is to be his second name." Uncle Leopold must have reminded her that she had him to thank for her matrimonial felicity (which was indeed true) but the bliss of it had expunged everything else from her mind, and again she wrote: "You will understand *how* fervent my prayers, and I am sure *everybody's* must be, to see him resemble his angelic dearest Father in *every every* respect, both in body and mind. Oh! my dearest Uncle, I am sure if you knew *how* happy, how blessed I feel, and how *proud* I feel in possessing such a perfect being as my husband, as he is, and if you think you have been instrumental in bringing about this union, it must gladden your heart!"

43

The Royal Family's first visit to Scotland in 1842: the
arrival at Aberdeen.

Pen and ink sketch by Queen Victoria of her four eldest
children at Osborne, July, 1846.

V · THE "ANGEL" AT WORK

UNTIL NOVEMBER 9, 1841 no male heir had been born to the Sovereign since the birth of George IV in 1762, and there were weighty points of procedure to be settled now which had not arisen then. Little Albert Edward was Earl of Chester from the moment he first drew breath, and within a month his mother created him Prince of Wales, but a heraldic battle raged over his Arms. His father had the right to the Arms of a Duke of Saxony and wished that his son should bear them quartered with the Arms of England. Since Albert wished it, the Queen ordered that this should be done, but it was not quite so simple. The Earl Marshal had to instruct the Herald's College to see that the coat was correct, and the Heralds strongly objected to the Royal Arms of England being quartered with those of so insignificant a realm: they pronounced it most derogatory to England. So the Queen wrote to say that such was her command, and the Heralds on behalf of the nation had to swallow the insult. Then was the infant to be prayed for in church as "The Prince of Wales," or "His Royal Highness the Prince of Wales"? Again his father had to be considered: Albert, though a Royal Highness as well as his son, was only

45

prayed for as "Prince Albert." So, liturgically, "The Prince of Wales," was settled on as being a sufficient identification for purposes of orison.

The Queen had been feeling "low" after her son's birth, and the family of four went to stay at George IV's Pavilion at Brighton for the sake of the bracing airs. One can imagine with how horrified an eye Albert, whose taste in architecture and mural decoration were soon to brighten the Isle of Wight, beheld the corridor of flamboyant dragons. The parents went back to London and in May the Queen gave a great fancy dress ball at which they appeared as Edward III and Queen Philippa. The sculptor Theed was commissioned to make life size statues of them in their picturesque costumes: these were the first of the Albert Marbles which presently grew so numerous.

This autumn (1842) the Queen and her husband visited Scotland for the first time. She was very proud of the Scotch blood that ran in her veins, and from now till the end of her life she was happiest in the Highlands. Her account of the tour bubbles with that excitement and vivid observation which new experiences always brought her. It started at Edinburgh, and they were escorted through the town at foot's pace by the Royal Archers, who, it thrilled her to learn, were a body of noblemen and gentlemen established by her remote ancestor James I of Scotland to form a personal bodyguard to the Sovereign of Scotland, and that was a wonderful inheritance! They stayed at Dalkeith with the Duke of Buc-cleuch (a distant and illegitimate relative through the Duke of Monmouth), and oatmeal porridge and Finnan haddock were new articles of diet. Albert was equally enthusiastic: he was sure that the Acropolis at Athens, though he had never seen it, could not be finer than Arthur's Seat, and Perth reminded him of Basle, and the view from Birnam Wood of his beloved Thüringen, and many of the people looked like Germans, so it all seemed homelike to his eye. He had his first experience of stalking, which, in spite of his previous reluctance to waste the shining hours in sport, he much enjoyed. "Without doubt," he wrote to Prince Charles of Leiningen, "deerstalking is one of the most fatiguing, but it is also one of the most interesting of pursuits," though it was a surprise to find that Scotch forests did not contain a single tree. The Queen duly noted his pleasure, and perhaps the fact that Lord Breadalbane's house "was a

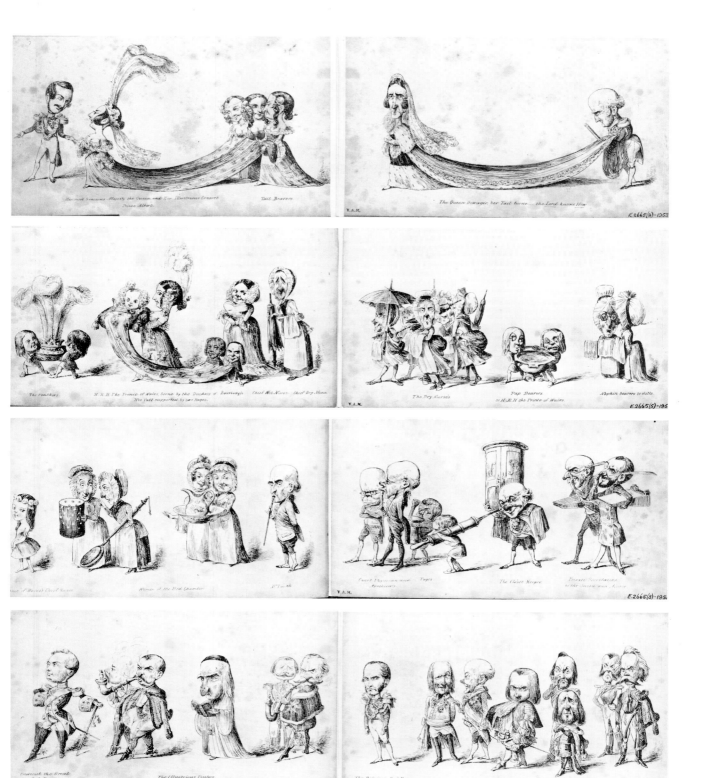

A satirical view: 'The Christening Procession of Prince
Taffy', published in 1842.

kind of Castle built of granite," contained the germ of a future scheme. There were sword-dances, there were bagpipes and feudalities, and kilts of Campbell tartan and Scotch reels, in which she and Albert (though dropping with fatigue after his deerstalking) took part. Altogether it was an enchanting holiday among these Highlands and "chivalrous, fine, active Highlanders"; there was a quiet, a retirement, a wildness, a liberty, and a solitude that had a tremendous charm for them both; and

Popular lithograph of the Royal Family leaving Windsor
by train.

the Queen wrote to Lord Melbourne, "We *must* come back for longer another time."

They travelled from London to Windsor by the railway which had not long been opened: to travel at all by this ferociously rapid means of transport (only three-quarters of an hour's journey) was still regarded as rather perilous, and prudent people saw that their wills were in order before they embarked. Hitherto when the Queen journeyed the Master of the Horse and the Royal coachman were in charge, but now they could be no more than passengers, with an engine-driver as coachman, and a guard for Master of the Horse. All was well at Windsor: Sarah, Lady Lyttelton was now in command of the Royal nurseries, and Vicky, also known as Pussie, had grown a great deal, and had become very independent. The baby, alas, was sadly backward for a child of ten months, but

Albert and Stockmar were already beginning to think about schemes for his education. "Education," said Stockmar, "begins at birth." Melbourne when consulted was not so encouraging. He thought that education rarely altered character. But then he was getting a little cynical: in answer to the Queen's enthusiasm about Scotland he had said that the drawback to that country was that the Scotch thought so highly of it.

It was now time for Lehzen to go. The Queen had two children already, and a third was coming, and there was no longer any place for her in the intimate domestic life. Moreover, the Queen, in her restored attachment with her mother had learned that in the unhappy dissensions of her youth, Lehzen, though always taking her part, had been mischievous, stirring up strife, instead of working for a better understanding: since her marriage also she had shewn herself jealous and interfering, as a middle-aged woman, once governess and confidante, is apt to do. Her significance, as the Invisible Woman behind the throne, corresponding to Stockmar the Invisible Man, was nothing more than a fable of gossip; she was a devoted, harmless old lady, growing tiresome, for whom, as she saw herself, there was no longer a place. The parting was perfectly friendly, and the Queen continued to write constantly to her in her home at Bückeburg, where she lived with her sister, for the rest of her life.

With Lehzen's departure, Stockmar could get on with his investigations into the domestic mismanagement of the Royal Households in London and at Windsor and on this subject he prepared the most exhaustive of his Memoranda up to date. Possibly Stockmar's sardonic pen got the better of him when he reported that if the Queen thought the dining-room cold the fire could not be lit without the co-operation of two departments, for we may be quite certain that if she wanted a fire it would have been lit in less than no time, but there was no question about the waste and the lack of a general control. Every day fresh candles, bouquets of them, were placed in all the living rooms, and whether they were used or not they were removed next day and became the perquisites of the footmen. There were forty housemaids at Windsor, and another forty at Buckingham Palace, so that these young ladies received board and lodging and £45 a year for six months' work. Footmen were employed in relays: one third were on duty, one third on half duty, and the remainder resting. Housemaids were in the province of the Lord Chamberlain, footmen in that of the Master of the Horse, cooks curtsied to the Lord Steward. Pointless extravagances were not wholly balanced by equally ludicrous economies: match boxes were scarce and there was a rule that no visitor should have more than two candles in his bedroom. So the ingenious Madame Tietjens, who was at Windsor to sing to the Queen, cut hers in half and made four, by the light of which she could dress.

The Prince having sufficiently mastered Stockmar's memorandum (it took time) went forward with reforms. This quadruple control of non-resident Officers of State was the first thing to remedy, and the Master of the Household was put in control of all departments. The Prince reduced the staff, he reduced their wages, he put an end to absurd perquisites and payments for long obsolete services. Perfectly unreasonable criticisms were showered on him for these excellent economies, as if waste was a virtue in exalted houses: he was cartooned creeping about to collect candle-ends. A more reasonable objection might be found to his appointment of Germans to responsible posts in the staff. The pages, for instance, were under the control of the German courier, Heller, and one day Master Kennaird wanted to throw him over the banisters . . .

The New Year of 1843 opened gaily at Windsor with two dances, and once more, as a year ago, Lord Melbourne stayed there. But the glamour had faded, and the Queen knew it. She *"almost* fancied happy old times were returned: but alas! the dream is past." She had awoke from it to a dawn brighter than any dreams, but to him it was not dawn to which he had awoke, but to an evening obscured by age and maladies. To Melbourne those three years, when every evening almost he had sat by her sofa, and made her laugh with his cynical or witty answers to her innumerable questions, had been of the quality of romance: but to her already, with Albert to shew her the better way, they seemed an idle profitless time.

She was expecting a third child, and she proposed to Sir Robert Peel that Albert should hold Levées for her. But she was anxious about the way her people would take that: perhaps it would be better that they should not kneel and kiss his hand, and it must be known that presentations to him would be equivalent to presentations to her. "*He* and *I*," she

Queen Victoria arriving at Château d'Eu during her visit
to the King of France in 1843.

wrote to Uncle Leopold, "must be one . . . and, God knows, he, dear angel, *deserves* to be the *highest in everything*." But her misgivings were justified, there was a great deal of unfriendly criticism, and the Levées were very poorly attended.

The Queen's third child Alice was born on April 25, 1843, and she thought it would be a friendly act to ask Uncle Ernest, King of Hanover, to be a godfather. There were risks, for who knew how the Ogre, as he was called, would behave? The King began badly: he arrived for the christening of Princess Alice at Buckingham Palace in a four-wheeler after the christening and the lunch that followed were over, and was annoyed they had not waited for him. "But," so the Queen wrote, "he was very gracious for *him*." The graciousness did not extend to Albert. The King asked him to come for a walk about the streets, but when Albert suggested that the crowds that would follow them would be an embarrassment, he said "I used to be much more unpopular than you, but I used to walk about with perfect impunity."

This summer the Queen for the first time left her native shores, and on the new yacht, inevitably named the *Victoria and Albert* and built and commissioned at the expense of the nation, she and her husband paid a visit to Louis Philippe King of France and father-in-law of Uncle Leopold at the Château d'Eu.

On their return to Brighton where the young family were occupying the Pavilion, they found Pussie was "amazingly advanced in intellect, but alas also in naughtiness," Bertie was much *embelli*, Alice (called Fatima because of her plumpness) was enormous and flourishing. For the rest of the autumn they paid visits in England. Prince Albert received the degree of Litt. D. at Cambridge, and the Queen saw with pleasure the enthusiasm with which the "rising generation" received him, but that was not to be wondered at, for she had noted before that "Albert always *fascinates* people wherever he goes by his very modest and unostentatious and dignified ways." They stayed at Chatsworth, where the sight of the colossal conservatory, built by Mr Joseph Paxton, made a great impression on the Prince – would it be possible to build even a larger glasshouse than that? – and to the Duke of Rutland's. Albert went out hunting with the Belvoir pack, and at last, at last, thought the Queen, some of these stupid people would see how truly English he was, for he rode admirably. "How well Albert's hunting answered!" she wrote to Uncle Leopold. It produced a sensation: the press all over the country made mention of it. They thought more highly of his seat on a horse than of his splendid speech to the manufacturers at Birmingham. Very absurd of them, no doubt, but she was tremendously pleased.

Whether the Queen really believed that Albert exercised this universal fascination is doubtful, for she alludes to the various manifestations of it with just such emphatic utterance as M. Coué recommended to his patients in order that their health might daily improve in consequence of their firm assertion that it was improving. Or perhaps she was so radically convinced of his perfections that she could scarcely conceive of others not recognising them. Who could help being warmed and gladdened by that brilliant sun? Basking in it herself, she thought that all her people must be basking in it, too, and what lustre her home life shed! "They say that no Sovereign was ever loved more than I am," she wrote, "and *this* because of our happy domestic home, and the good example it

The earliest known photograph of Queen Victoria, with the Princess Royal, circa 1844–45.

presents." Sometimes her happiness so overwhelmed her that nothing else appeared of any consequence, and after a week of holiday at Claremont away from all cares of State, she wrote to Uncle Leopold: "God knows *how willingly* I would *always* live with my beloved Albert and his children in the quiet and retirement of private life." That was an utterly sincere and delightful sentiment, but was it a true one? Being Queen of England was as much part of her identity as being Albert's wife.

Then for a while, happily very brief, the Queen's domestic felicity was shattered. Duke Ernest, her father-in-law, died suddenly in January 1844, and though she had only come into touch with him for two short periods, once when he came to England with his sons in 1836, and for the second time at her wedding, she wrote to Uncle Leopold of the crushing, the overwhelming blow. He had been a father to her: "his like we shall *not see again*:" and she added a strange reflection for a blissfully happy wife, which was to prove vitally true hereafter: "Indeed one loves to *cling* to one's grief." All this was quite sincere, for he was Albert's father and though Albert had not seen him for four years, and in that interval had found him extremely trying, filial piety, the thought of the old home and the days of boyhood rendered it right to be broken-hearted. But for the Queen there was a further reason, not less sincere, for an even more poignant anguish. Albert felt it would comfort him to go to Coburg, where he could be of use to his brother, and she could not go with him, imposing a Sovereign's presence in the house of mourning. She had said after her marriage that a parting between her and Albert "*will and shall never happen*, for I would go with him even if he was to go to the *North Pole*," and though he was not going to the North Pole, he was going to Coburg, and she would be left alone. Could Aunt Louise and Uncle Leopold come to stay with her, and help her to bear the intolerable? . . . "I have never been separated from him," she wrote, "even for *one night*, and the *thought of such* a separation is quite dreadful . . . still, I feel I could bear it – I have made up my mind to it, as the very *thought* of going has been a comfort to my poor Angel and will be of such use at Coburg. Still, if I were to remain *quite* alone, I do not think I *could* bear it quietly . . . I may be indiscreet, but you must think of *what* the separation from my *all and all*, even only for a fortnight will be to me! We feel some *years* older since these days of mourning."

So Uncle Leopold and Aunt Louise hastened over to England, and Victoria was parted from her husband for the first time. He quite appreciated what his absence meant to her, and wrote with encouraging consolation before embarking at Dover; "Poor child! You will while I write be getting ready for luncheon, and you will find a place vacant, where I sat yesterday . . . You are even now half a day nearer to seeing me again: by the time you get this you will be a whole one – thirteen more and I am again within your arms" . . . But what a joy it was for the *treue Coburger* to be at home again after four years' absence! "How lovely and friendly," he wrote, "is this dear old country, how glad I should be to have my little wife beside me, that I might share my pleasures with her"; and he sent her pressed flowers, gathered at Rosenau where he was born. Assuredly he was very fond of her: he recognised that their union was of "heart and soul and therefore noble," but we miss somehow the craving of the lover for the beloved. Or did he suppress that, lest her heart should be wrung by his suffering? If so, his knowledge of women was most elementary, for nothing would have given her a more ecstatic anguish than to know how desolate was his loneliness. So she ticked off the days of his absence, and, as he impersonally noted, there was "great Joy," when he got back to Windsor.

Tsar Nicholas I of Russia proposed himself for a visit to England this summer. The Queen considered it a great compliment and was rather snobbish about it. She "found it like a dream to breakfast and walk out with *this* greatest of all earthly Potentates as quietly as if we walked etc. with Charles or anyone." He had an uncivilised mind, she thought, he was sadly lacking in education and was quite insensible to the Arts, but he was very easy to get on with, and the children were not shy of him. He was extremely polite, he said of Windsor "C'est digne de vous, Madame," and he had an eye for a pretty woman, which reminded her of Uncle's little ways. Best of all he was full of praise for her Angel: Albert had "l'air si noble et si bon," and the Queen hoped that he would repeat these gratifying remarks abroad, for, coming from him, they would have great weight.

These Royal visits, by which the Queen set great store, multiplied. With the Tsar came the King of Saxony: he was no bother at all, for he

went out sight-seeing all day and was "*so* unassuming." In August came Prince William of Prussia, brother of the reigning King and later Emperor William I of Germany, and in October King Louis Philippe and his son the Duc de Montpensier. The King's dietetic and other requirements, enumerated to the Queen by his daughter Aunt Louise, were somewhat complicated. He must not be allowed to come down to breakfast or he would certainly eat something, which was bad for him the first thing in the morning, but he must have a bowl of chicken broth a little later. He must have a hard bed, a horse-hair mattress laid on a plank if possible, and a large table for his papers. An eye must be kept on him for fear of his catching cold, and though he was sending horses to England, he must not be allowed to ride, and if he went to London or Woolwich, as he much wished to do, he must go by train.

These precautions being duly observed, the visit was most successful. The King was enthusiastically received, he thoroughly enjoyed himself and the Queen's favourable impression of him was intensified. He was very friendly about an awkward *fracas* that there had lately been

The monarchs of Europe: Victoria and Albert with
Louis-Philippe and Marie-Amélie of France and Leopold
and Louise of Belgium.

between the French and English at Tahiti, he expressed his determination to see the Queen every year in the future, and best of all he appreciated "my *dearest* master's" great qualities and talents, treating him as an equal, "calling him 'Mon Frère' and saying that my husband was the same as me, which it is – and 'Le Prince Albert, c'est pour moi le Roi.'" These Royal visits were very popular in the country: the Queen was being magnificent in her entertainment of the Kings of the earth (and that is what a Queen should be), and the nation, after the monstrous extravagances of her Uncles was pleased to be told that every penny of the expense was borne, without incurring debt, by the Queen's private purse. Albert's admirable economies in the Royal houses were already fruitful.

In August, between Royal visits her fourth child Prince Alfred was born, and the family was beginning to grow *nombreuse* in spite of her earlier sentiments on the subject. It was fairly certain now that Ernest, the reigning Duke of Coburg, whose marriage had restored him to favour with Albert, would have no children, and thus, after Ernest's death, Albert's children would succeed to the Dukedom. Bertie, as heir to the English Crown, could not inherit, and the new baby was the immediate heir. Though the infant was an English Prince the spirit of *der treue Coburger* in his father expressed itself emphatically. "The little one," he wrote to his brother, "shall from his youth be taught to love the small dear country to which he belongs *in every respect*, as does his Papa."

The Queen longed for some more private and intimate stage for the domestic life which was the chief source of her abounding happiness than Windsor and Buckingham Palace afforded, one that should be "free from all Woods and Forest and other charming Departments who really are the plague of one's life." As a small girl she had twice stayed with her mother at Norris Castle in the Isle of Wight, near to Osborne Cottage, where Sir John Conroy lived. She liked the place, and in 1843 Sir Robert Peel had been set to make confidential enquiries about buying the Osborne Estate, prudently concealing the name of the prospective purchaser for fear of the price being put up, and early in 1845 she bought some eight hundred acres, including Osborne House. It was not nearly big enough for the parents and the growing family and the visiting

Ministers, but they entertained the King of Holland there. As Prince William of Orange he had been William IV's candidate in 1836 for the hand of Victoria, and she recorded with some complacency the astonishing change he found between the little Princess, "crushed and kept under," and hardly daring to speak a word, "and the independent and unembarrassed Queen." He had lost all his front teeth, but thought she had grown . . .

Self-portrait of 1845, just before Victoria's 26th
birthday.

The new house was at once begun, and Albert exhibited fresh and amazing talents. He drew the plans for it, subject to the revision of Mr Thomas Cubitt to whom London owes so much that is solidly residential in the west-end. He visualized the Clock Tower and the Flag Tower and the open colonnade, he laid out the grounds with their two terraces and their miles of winding roads with "blicks" of the sea. Then, sunburnt with landscape-gardening, and flushed with climbing ladders, he turned the full beam of his taste on the internal decorations and furnishings. There were alcoves painted Garter-blue, surrounded by borders of sea-shells in plaster and in the alcoves were bronze busts and statues of the Coburg family, and English sculptors, Thorneycroft and Theed and

Edgar Boehm were busy producing more and yet more of the Albert Marbles, starting with the group of him and the Queen as Edward III and Philippa, and another of the Prince in Roman armour. There was more intimate statuary as well as these public pieces, for the Queen had marble models made of the hands or the feet of her young family. The Prince had a great admiration for fresco: to him it was the noblest form of painting. So Mr. W. Dyce, R.A. set forth on the walls of the staircase a huge representation of Neptune (surrounded by a hierarchy of nude gods and goddesses), giving the Empire of the Sea to Britannia, and on the walls of the Prince's dressing-room and bathroom the allegorical and allusive scene of the marriage of Hercules and Omphale. There were two chairs hewn out of solid blocks of coal, for mining was the greatest of English industries and, later, there were other chairs of which the legs and framework consisted of the horns of stags which the Prince had shot in the deer forests of Balmoral. Admirable pictures by Winterhalter of the parents and young family frolicking round them multiplied on the walls, and of dogs and deer by Landseer and of Albert returned from shooting and Victoria standing by him admiring the mixed bag of feather and fur laid out on the carpet. There were statuettes of dogs and ponies and favourite Highland gillies, and "porcelain views." This remarkable form of reminiscent art was introduced by Prince Albert from Germany: famous views were painted below glaze on plates and teapots, glimpses of Rosenau or the Thuringian forest. He adapted this form to domestic memorial pieces, and Eos and the Queen's dogs with their names for identification lived again in china. Etchings were executed by the Royal pair, and there were stacks of lithographs of the family pictures.

By the time the estate was bought and the new home furnished, the cost had been not less than £200,000. The Pavilion at Brighton had been sold to the Corporation, which furnished some fraction of the expense, but otherwise every penny of this sum was paid out of the Queen's private purse. There had been many large expenses as well; £70,000 had been spent over the new stables at Windsor and Buckingham Palace, Royalty had been frequently and sumptuously entertained. Once more the Prince had shewn himself a master in the management of money.

Early photograph of Balmoral, rising above the River Dee.

Tartan fabrics and thistle-patterned wallpaper in the
drawing room at Balmoral. Watercolour by J. ROBERTS.

Illustration from the catalogue of the Great Exhibition,
showing a vast malachite vase from St Petersburg.

vi · The Great Exhibition

Fresh fields had presented themselves for the Prince's activities, and none was too small for cultivation, and none too large. He noticed, for instance, that many posts in the English church, like Cathedral canonries, were sinecures: would it not be well to fill them up with scholars who were doing research work? At his instigation the Queen wrote to the Prime Minister calling his attention to the claims of Mr Cureton who had translated the Epistle of St Ignatius from the Syriac, and was about to translate the Gospel of St Matthew from the original Coptic. A large field adjoined that, and in pursuance of the promotion of education the Prince in 1847 stood for the Chancellorship of Cambridge University. It shocked the Queen that, if he was willing to accept it, there should be any other candidate, but Lord Powis had the disloyalty to oppose him and was well punished by being heavily defeated. The Queen went up to Cambridge to see Albert confer honorary degrees on disting-uished people, and he read an address of welcome to her and after dinner they walked through the courts of Trinity in a state of high romance. Then he set to work to examine the educational curriculum of the ancient University, for he never allowed any office that he held to be a sinecure to him, and found it to be deplorably narrow. Classics and mathematics seemed the only subjects taught there: it was a place of darkness rather than enlightenment, and not a patch on the Universities of his Fatherland. Within a year's time he had worked out a scheme for comprehensive reform, introducing into his programme such subjects as chemistry, psychology, and modern languages, and the place of darkness received it with great cordiality.

Prince Albert, in his role as Chancellor of Cambridge
University, presents an address to the Queen.

Education, enlightenment . . . These to the Prince's mind, which in its conceptions was idealistic and in its methods Teutonically logical, were the panaceas for all the warring disquietudes of the world, and his imagination reached out to far vaster parishes. He saw that with all this revolutionary yeast bubbling abroad, and with his impetuous Foreign Secretary ready to knead the perilous loaf at home, the peace of Europe might at any time be endangered, and that the surest way of averting a cataclysm was to prove to the unquiet nations that the prosperity of each was wrapped up with the industrial prosperity of others. The world's progress was an indivisible unit and it was for England to demonstrate that. There must be a monster Exhibition in London, at which should be displayed all the products of the civilised world, and thus the nations would see that in the lucrative arts of peace rather than in the destructive panoply of war lay their moral and material salvation. To use his own definition, which precisely stated what he had in view: "The Exhibition of 1851 is to give us a true test and a living picture of the point of development at which the whole of mankind has arrived in this great task of applied science and a new starting-point from which all nations will be able to direct their further exertions." Though his detached mind left out of consideration the factor of human passion (for when two nations are on the verge of a quarrel they will not pause to think whether, by pressing it, their supplies of butter or bedsteads from abroad will be cut off), his idea was admirable, and he was the initiator of the great exhibitions which ever since have proved so strong an incentive to industrial progress and the expansion of trade.

The Prince outlined his scheme to a few members of the Society of Arts, and on their approval devoted to it all his amazing powers of organization. The first step was to get hold of English manufacturers and captains of industries: they would surely see that such an Exhibition would give them a prodigious advertisement for their goods, and that while it promoted the cause of world-amity it would also be the shareholders' friend. At a dinner at the Mansion House he addressed eighty-two Mayors of provincial towns in industrial districts and thus secured the municipal support of local centres. But England was only the foundation of the structure he proposed to raise: to realise his design all foreign nations must join hands in this comradeship of progressive and inter-dependent industry. Greenland's icy mountains must send bear-skins, and India's coral strand pearls and elephant-tusks, and China its porcelain and Spain its tapestries and Switzerland its chocolate and cuckoo-clocks. Distinguished Ambassadors must attend officially; Buckingham Palace would welcome the Royalties, and local hosts would entertain other representatives: Liverpool would show them the new Albert Dock, and Cardiff its coal-mines and Staffordshire its potteries. All looked very promising.

But the bright dream of this cosmopolitan temple of industries where all nations would worship grew dark. The year 1848 had seen thrones

Length of printed cotton, made to commemorate the
1851 Great Exhibition, showing the Crystal Palace, then
in Hyde Park.

totter and heard the blare of revolutionary trumpets, and the foreign potentates who were bidden to the celebration were apprehensive that this august assembly would provide the foes of Kings with an unrivalled opportunity for a *battue*. Then the bright dream became nightmare, for a storm of opposition sprang up in England itself. It was largely directed against the Prince personally and an organized attack was launched in the press and in Parliament. Funds were short: it was argued that a mob of Continental revolutionists would be let loose on London, and Albert, almost despairing, wrote to his brother to say that he expected that he would have to give it up. But still he worked on, the Queen was behind him, and so were the industrial centres. The tide turned, money came in, Parliament sanctioned the site which had been chosen in Hyde Park, and Albert unrolled again the sheaves of architectural designs for the building. One particularly took his fancy, for he remembered going to Chatsworth some years ago and being immensely struck by the gigantic conservatory built there by Mr Joseph Paxton. Both the Queen and he

Victoria and Albert opening the Great Exhibition on
1 May, 1851.

thought it "out and out the finest thing imaginable of its kind": it was
300 feet long and 64 feet high, so that the tropical trees within did not
nearly reach the roof; and now Mr Paxton had sent in a design on the
same lines but of far vaster scale, a conservatory a thousand feet long, all
of glass, like the New Jerusalem, erected on frames and girders of iron
painted bright blue, and so high that it would be unnecessary to clear the
site of the few trees that stood there. Mr Paxton's design was accepted.
Within such an edifice there would be room for all the assembled
inventions of progressive civilization, and as soon as the Crystal Palace
was ready they poured into it: masses of machinery and oil-yielding
palms, stuffed elephants with immense ivory tusks, locomotives, stamps
for crushing ores, the pit head of a coal mine, Persian carpets and
Kidderminster rugs, porcelain and wax flowers and glass paper weights
and bedsteads and blankets – it must suffice to say that nothing was
omitted which could serve to draw the nations together by the bonds of
industry and applied science. The pacific influence of the Arts was

65

represented also: a vast organ, that noblest of musical instruments, was built in the concert hall, there was a picture-gallery, there were stained glass windows for sacred art, and for profane an Olympus of the casts of Greek statues and of Egyptian bas-reliefs, and Mr Tennyson the new poet-laureate, though fallaciously assigning the glory of the completed scheme to the Queen, summed up, in an address to her, the conception and the fulfilment of Prince Albert's dream:

> "She brought a vast design to pass
> When Europe and the scattered ends
> Of our fierce world did meet as friends
> And brethren in her halls of glass."

The Exhibition was opened on May 1, 1851. The Prince and Princess of Prussia and their son Frederick, then aged twenty, braved the risk of assassination, and for the first time the young man set eyes on that lively intelligent girl of ten who spoke German as fluently as English, and who, seven years hence, was to bring Coburg blood into the House of Prussia. As for the Exhibition itself, the ravens who croaked disaster and discouragement were dumb, for from the day of its opening till it closed in October it was a seething mass of enchanted visitors; while as for the Queen, she was even as the Queen of Sheba, bewildered and "quite beaten" with the beauty and the vastness of it. "A fairy scene: the *greatest* day in our history. Many cried and all felt touched and impressed with devotional feelings. It was the *happiest, proudest* day in my life." She had indeed the right to feel like that, for it was Albert's own conception, and he had triumphantly carried it through by two years of incessant work in the face of innumerable difficulties. Day after day she visited it in the early morning, and every visit confirmed her enthusiasm. The financial results exceeded all expectations: £200,000 had been guaranteed, but the guarantors were not called upon to put down a penny: instead, a profit of £186,000 was realized, or 93% over and above the sum guaranteed. Indeed the Prince had the Midas touch, and, when all was settled up, the Commissioners, on his recommendation, bought thirty acres of land round about the present Exhibition Road in Kensington for £50,000. Those who are curious in such matters may compute from the value of freeholds there to-day, what the appreciation of that purchase has been.

That site, too, was to serve the cause of education, and on it now stand a score of museums and establishments for the furtherance of Arts and Sciences, and the great Hall built in memory of him from whom the whole idea sprang.

The Queen's love for her husband and her admiration for his character could scarcely rise higher, but this really immense achievement enhanced her sense of his gifts to the depreciation of her own. Both in politics and business he showed "such perspicacity, such *courage*." "We women," she wrote to her Uncle Leopold, "are not *made* for governing – and if we are good women we must *dislike* these masculine occupations." She had to reiterate that, and again she wrote that, though she was interested in European politics, "I am every day more convinced that *we women* if we are to be *good* women, *feminine* and *amiable* and *domestic* are *not fitted to reign*." A strange *volte-face*: as a young girl with Melbourne by her side she had shouldered the duties of Sovereignty without a qualm of misgiving: now, with Albert by her side, and fourteen years of experience behind her, she announced her virtual abdication. As for him, he had become "such a *terrible* man of business" that she wondered whether these preoccupations took a little off from the gentleness of his character . . .

After the creation of his Exhibition, Albert was soon busy again creating a new home. Two entrancing visits to Scotland had determined the Queen to have a house in the Highlands and in 1848 she had taken a lease of Balmoral, a small Scotch Castle on Deeside. It was inconveniently small for the growing family and the Household and the Ministers in attendance; the latter had only a billiard-room as a joint sitting-room, but the Queen revelled in its remoteness and privacy. Albert had admitted that deerstalking was the most interesting of pursuits, and the Queen went out with him, and after the excitement was over, good Grant or Macdonald made tea in some sheltered nook, and the kettle wouldn't boil, and John Brown told her she would be wise to put on her waterproof. They picnicked, they stayed in remote bothies and played dummy whist after dinner; they made incognito tours through wild districts staying in primitive inns and eating tough chickens with no potatoes. They made friends with the charming gillies who accompanied them, and Albert had lessons in Gaelic: "a very difficult language for it is pronounced in a totally different way from that in which it is written." When not out with Albert on the hill, the Queen visited the houses of the crofters and took them flannel petticoats, and made small purchases in village shops. In other words they lived like a conscientious homely couple on holiday at their country estate, looking after their tenants as good landlords should. Even Greville who never lost an opportunity to disparage and ridicule them could spy no target for his acidities when in

Queen Victoria's watercolour of Maggie Gow, daughter
of one of the tenants at Balmoral.

1849 he was summoned to Balmoral for a Council and found only a charming simplicity and ease "as of gentlefolk." The Queen was busy all day with her duties and her errands, and after dinner she and the Prince went back to the cleared dining-room and had a dancing lesson in Scotch reels, while the Prime Minister and he played billiards. Here the Prince laid aside all his dignity and stiffness, he made puns, he roared with laughter if somebody tripped over a rumpled hearth-rug: the witty Lord Granville used to say that he never told his best stories, when pretending to pinch your finger in the door was so much more effective.

But the house had soon been found not spacious enough even for this refreshing and simple existence, and after four years the Queen bought the estate, and Albert, with the architectural experience of Osborne behind him, made his plans for something more Schloss-like, built of granite, and in 1855 the new Castle was habitable. Inside, in recognition of the Queen's Scotch ancestry, tartans flowered on the walls and the carpets and the furniture, Balmoral tartan, and Victoria tartan and Royal Stuart tartan. Family busts and statues accumulated, the walls grew spiky with the trophies of the Prince's stalking and the neighbouring hills with the cairns that commemorated important events. To the Queen, as

Queen Victoria sketching at Loch Loggan with her two
eldest children, 1857; after a painting by LANDSEER.

the towers soared and the tartans and the gardens blossomed Balmoral became far more than a refuge from the fierce light and the cares of State, where she could enjoy the domestic felicity for which, as she had once told Uncle Leopold, she would be fain to have done with Sovereignty. It became a symbol of its creator, who was the core of her happiness, and when the "poor old house" had vanished, and the new Castle with its towers and pinnacles and its gilt sculptured coats of arms gleamed in the late light, she wrote: "Every year my heart becomes more fixed in this dear Paradise, and so much more now, that *all* has become my dear Albert's *own* creation, own work, own building, own laying out, as at Osborne, and his great taste and the impress of his dear hand have been stamped everywhere."

Lord Palmerston, foreign minister and later Prime
Minister, for whom Victoria felt some antagonism.

Victoria distributing the Crimean Medals at the Horse
Guards, 18 May 1856.

VII · POLITICS AND WAR

THE QUEEN'S OBJECTION to Lord Palmerston, her Foreign Minister at this time, was of the very strongest, for, unlike Melbourne, unlike Peel and Aberdeen, he had no respect for the Prince's opinions and no patience with his careful, his logical, his admirably reasoned and, it must be added, his interminable memoranda. "To me," the Prince once said to the Queen, "a long closely connected train of reasoning is like a beautiful strain of music. You can scarcely imagine my delight." But, equally, he could not imagine Palmerston's impatience with these beautiful strains of music. Palmerston despised the Prince's reasoned and logical reviews as applied to the cut and thrust of international politics as thoroughly as the Prince was appalled at the Foreign Secretary's summary methods of handling crises. Crises, he said, were liable to arise suddenly and must be dealt with summarily: there was no time for symphonies. Neither of them, though extremely able men, could see the merits of the other's technique. To Palmerston, the Prince's mind was a fit instrument only for an editor of St Ignatius's epistles: Palmerston's mind, thought the Prince, was that of a gambler at the poker-table, where bluff was a valuable weapon. Neither did justice to the other, for some crises are best solved by such reasoning as gave the Prince symphonic pleasure, others by a poker face. Palmerston, moreover, seemed to enjoy perilous positions; it added savour to his cigar to smoke it in a powder-magazine.

To the Queen any criticism of her husband's views was now almost of the nature of blasphemy. She looked upon him as wisdom incarnate, and in all questions from the decorations at Osborne to the unification of Germany she identified herself with him. He was the Crown. But Palmerston often did worse than criticize him: he ignored him. He disagreed with all the Prince's views on international politics, and he did not bother his head to discuss them with him. Once when he spent a day with the Prince out stalking, the latter was hopeful that the Foreign Secretary was impressed by his solid reasoning on some such topic. But he was wrong: Palmerston let him have it his own way because it was not worth while to argue with the man. He really might be called an atheist.

Lord John Russell, then Prime Minister, had the impossible task of trying to keep peace between his Foreign Minister and the Queen. He knew how enormous was Palmerston's, not the Prince's popularity in the country, and that any Government which quarrelled with him risked its existence. He knew, too (though he could never tell her that), that the Prince, in spite of the success of his Exhibition, was now, more than ever, regarded as a foreigner, who, by virtue of his domination of her, was reckoned a far greater danger to the country than any antics of her Foreign Minister. Indeed Palmerston's unpopularity with the Crown might be considered an inverse barometrical reading of his general popularity: the stormier the presage of the weather in one respect, the more settled was the weather in the other. Lord John, though suffering sharply himself from Palmerston's contumacy did all he could to reconcile the irreconcilables: he wrote soft answers to the sarcastic and censorious notes the Queen volleyed at him as if he had himself been guilty of Palmerston's "wilful indiscretions," but never an atom of her wrath did he turn away.

There came a brief respite from Palmerston's squibs and pin-pricks. On December 2, 1851, Prince Louis Napoleon, President of the French Republic, brought off his military *coup d'état* in Paris. Both the Queen and the Cabinet highly disapproved of such bloodshed and violence, and

Palmerston was instructed to write to Lord Normanby, British Ambassador in Paris, that England was maintaining a strict neutrality. But on his own account he expressed to Count Walewski, French Ambassador in London, his "entire approbation of the act of the President." Count Walewski communicated this to his Government, and thus England was in the awkward position of having simultaneously expressed her approval and of having declared neutrality. Lord John therefore asked Palmerston for explanations, and since they were quite unsatisfactory, he dismissed him from his post of Foreign Secretary, the Cabinet concurring.

To the Queen and the Prince this came as a complete and delightful surprise, and needless to say the Prime Minister incurred no reproof for taking so unconstitutional a step without the consent of the Crown. He had done what they had hopelessly failed to do for years, and their joy bubbled over. The Queen wrote to Uncle Leopold announcing the glad tidings (it was Christmas) which would give satisfaction "to the *whole* of the world." She chortled: "'The veteran statesman,' as the newspapers, to *our* great amusement, and I am sure to *his* infinite annoyance, call him, must rest upon his laurels." Albert, in an exultation of mixed metaphors, wrote to brother Ernest that the man who had embittered their whole lives had cut his own throat, and since he had been given enough rope had hanged himself. Having committed this double suicide surely he must be dead!

But he was never more alive, nor less resting on his laurels: there were many more to be added. Two months later he brought about the defeat of the Government in the House of Commons; Lord John Russell resigned, and the Queen called upon Lord Derby to form a Ministry. The only historical interest about its transitory life was that Disraeli took office as Chancellor of the Exchequer. Hitherto he had been in the Queen's blackest books for the bitter suavity of his attacks on the late Sir Robert Peel. But now she began to feel differently about him. She found his financial statements very clear and able and his reports on Parliamentary business were really amusing: he wrote to her of a debate "languishing with successive relays of mediocrity, until it yielded its last gasp in the arms of Mr Slaney." This was quite a new style, and he was a new kind of statesman, with his rococo manner and his Oriental flamboyance. But his tenure of office was short: the July elections declared against the Government and in the winter they were defeated over Disraeli's budget. Lord Aberdeen then undertook to form a Coalition Government of Whigs, Peelites and Liberals, but he could not do without Palmerston who re-entered the Cabinet as Home Secretary within a year of the time when the Queen and the Prince had rejoiced over his extinction. Gladstone succeeded Disraeli as Chancellor of the Exchequer: his first Budget

'*Les Défenseurs du Droit et de la Liberté de l'Europe*':
Franz Joseph of Austria, Abdul Medjid of Turkey,
Victoria and Napoleon III of France.

speeches roused so much enthusiasm (though Income Tax remained at the high rate of sevenpence in the pound for incomes over £150) that the Prince hoped that his Christian humility would not allow him to become dangerously elated.

In February 1854, England, with France as her ally, declared war on Russia in defence of Turkey. Quite early in her reign, when reviewing her Guards, the Queen had declared that she longed to lead her soldiers against her country's foes, and that essential valour was hers still: but since her presence at the head of her army in the Crimea would have been even more embarrassing than that of her *bon frère* the Emperor of the French, who threatened to do the same, she devoted herself to activities at home. She saw her troops off at daybreak: she embarked on her yacht and literally led out her fleet for the Baltic from Spithead: she offered her yacht as a transport for troops: she demanded to know, from the harassed Duke of Newcastle the exact effective numbers of muskets, Artillery, Infantry and Cavalry, militia, seamen and ammunition available in England for purposes of defence: she remonstrated with Lord Aberdeen because he deprecated the violent attacks in the English press on Russian perfidy and the character of the Tsar. Russia was an enemy, and it did not become her Prime Minister to be "impartial": this was not the time for impartiality. Her spirit was exactly that of her predecessor Queen Elizabeth, who, like her, always did her best to avoid war, but when forced to it, became Bellona incarnate. She would not hear of a "*day of humiliation*" being liturgically observed, for probably allusion would be made "to the *great sinfulness of the nation*, which brought about the war." Sheer hypocrisy! It was the sinfulness and ambition of the Tsar which were to blame. Have a day of prayer by all means, thanking God for the great prosperity of her people, and asking the help of the Almighty, but the thought of a day of humiliation was repulsive.

Throughout 1854 the war overshadowed all other interests: "We are," she wrote to Uncle Leopold, "and indeed the whole country is, *entirely* engrossed with one idea, one *anxious* thought – the *Crimea*." The victories at the Alma in September, and at Balaklava and Inkerman in the next two months were matters for rejoicing, but the end of the war could not be within sight till Sebastopol fell. A false report of that reached Balmoral in the autumn and a great bonfire was built to be lit when it was confirmed, but no confirmation came and for a year it remained unlit. Winter came on, and it became known how abjectly deficient were the commissariat departments, and how lamentable the state of the hospital at Scutari, into which Miss Florence Nightingale was now beginning to introduce the first elements of hygiene and nursing.

The outcry against this monstrous incompetence led to the resignation of Lord Aberdeen early in 1855, and for a while politics intruded themselves, for a most disconcerting contingency had to be faced. There

Queen Victoria's Coalition Ministry of 1855 included
Gladstone, Russell, Palmerston, Grey, Newcastle and
Grenville.

was only one man in the country who could keep a Ministry together,
and finally she sent for Palmerston. He accepted with alacrity, and within
a week's time of his forming his Government, he paid a visit to the
Emperor Napoleon at Paris, and blithely told the Queen that they
intended to correspond. There was consternation at Windsor: "How,"
asked Albert in a perturbed Memorandum, "can the Foreign Secretary
and Ambassador at Paris, the legitimate organ of communication, carry
on their business if everything has been previously preconcerted between
the Emperor and the English Prime Minister?" But as usual, Palmerston
took no notice of these perturbations.

As for the lately distrusted Emperor Napoleon III she cultivated the
friendliest relations with him. At the cost of bitter though brief bereavement she insisted on Albert's paying a four days' visit to him in his
military camp at St Omer, and the Emperor's gratifying appreciation of

The triumphal entry of Queen Victoria and Prince
Albert into Paris, 1855.

his "qualités si séduisantes et de connaissances si profondes" exting-
uished the last smoulderings of her distrust, and she invited him and the
Empress to stay with her at Windsor the following spring.

The Emperor and Empress had a great popular reception as they passed
through London on their State visit, and he pointed out to her the modest
house in King Street where he had lived when England was his place of
refuge; to-day Windsor received the exile on his Imperial return with the
highest honours. As for the Emperor he inspired the Queen with an
uneasy fascination: it was impossible not to feel warmly to a man who
had said that the irreproachable domestic felicity of his hostess had
raised the tone of the Courts of Europe, and that Albert was a Prince
among Princes, but had the Emperor, she asked herself (or Albert asked
her) "a strong *moral* sense of right and *wrong*?" He believed in his

"Star," in the Destiny God had imposed on him, which must be ruthlessly followed. And how picturesque it was that the granddaughter of George III should be dancing a quadrille with the nephew of England's arch-enemy, Napoleon I, in the Waterloo Room! She found the Empress Eugénie then in the height of her amazing beauty "very pretty and very uncommon-looking," which was a sound judgment.

The Emperor was very eager to cement these cordial relations, and in

The Royal Family at Balmoral in 1855. During this visit it was arranged that Prince Frederick William of Prussia (SECOND LEFT) should marry the Princess Royal (FAR RIGHT).

August the Queen and Prince Albert with their two eldest children returned the visit. Paris greeted them with the utmost enthusiasm: every day they were received with such ovations as had scarcely been accorded to Napoleon I returning from his foreign campaigns. She had never been in Paris before (nor indeed had any English Sovereign since Henry VI), and she was "*delighted, enchanted, amused* and *interested.*" Words failed her: their entry was quite *feenhaft* and *overpowering*, and she could but feebly express her emotions when she wrote to Uncle Leopold that "all old enmities and rivalries were *wiped out* over the tomb of Napoleon I, by whose coffin I stood (by torchlight) at the arm of Napoleon III now my nearest and dearest ally." There was no-one to whom she felt more inclined to talk unreservedly, or in whom she would be more inclined to confide . . . "he *has* the power of *attaching* those to him who come near him which is *quite incredible*." Albert, she allowed, was less enthusiastic, but the Emperor's feelings were "very reciprocal." The Empress was kind and good, but they saw little of her, "as for *really* and *certainly very* good reasons she must take great care of herself . . ."

The fascination of the Emperor and the Queen's conviction that the Anglo-French alliance was "completely sealed," was too optimistic: she revised her opinion before long and before long she reversed it. Far more significant for the destinies of Europe was the impression made on her thirteen-year-old son. Bertie was fascinated too: he wore his Stuart kilt, he knelt at the tomb of Napoleon, he took part in these great fêtes, Paris thought his manners charming, and to Paris he lost his heart. The childish impression was never effaced: he was already a little *boulevardier* with bare knees, and when the horrid moment came after ten blissful days to get back to his lessons and his tutors he begged the Empress to let him and his sister stay on for a little: Papa and Mamma had plenty of children at home, and they would not mind. There was also present at some of these fêtes a big moustached German. He was in Paris again fifteen years later, but the palace of St Cloud where the Queen was so royally lodged was no longer at the disposition of her host. The Germans had occupied it.

The new Castle at Balmoral was occupied for the first time this year (1855). It was Albert's creation and all, within and without, was perfection. The bonfire built in a hurry last year on the false report of the fall of Sebastopol had been upset by a November gale on the day of the victory at Inkerman, which to the Queen's keen eye for coincidence was very strange, and seemed (that was strange, too) "to wait for our return to be lit." It all came true, nor had it long to wait, for three days after her arrival in September came the authentic news and after dinner Albert with all the Household and staff climbed the hill, built it again and fired it. Dancing Highlanders surrounded it, whisky flowed, pipers played, and there was general ecstasy.

Fresh domestic excitement followed, for the Queen had purposefully bidden to Balmoral young Prince Frederick William of Prussia. He had asked the Queen's consent to propose to the little English Princess Royal. His parents approved, his uncle the King of Prussia approved, and the young lady's parents approved very much indeed, for he was a most admirable young man, and Vicky would have an excellent husband: also both the Queen and Prince Albert cherished the idea of the unification of Germany of which their daughter would one day be Queen, and the House of Coburg would be again enlarged by the acquisition of yet another crown.

By now the end of the war was in sight, and the Queen was very busy

The Princess Royal, with her parents, on her wedding
day, 25 January, 1858.

over the honours to be bestowed in connection with it. There were to be medals to be distributed personally to her returning soldiers, not officers alone but privates, to reward their gallant deeds. For those of conspicuous valour, officers and privates alike, she instituted the Victoria Cross, which as a Decoration she ranked above all that she could confer. There were details to be settled about it, in which we may certainly trace the precise mind of Albert. She thought the motto "For Valour" was better than "For the Brave" as the latter would lead to the inference "that only those are deemed brave who have got the Victoria Cross." To the admirable Miss Nightingale, the Queen sent an autograph letter and a brooch bearing her crown and cypher and a St George's Cross in red enamel with the inscription "Crimea. Blessed are the Merciful."

With the shadowing anxiety of the war removed, all the Queen's early gaiety shone forth again. She had always loved dancing, and though now growing stout and the mother of eight children she became almost *débutante* again with the *début* of her eldest daughter. Prince Albert always hated late hours but many a time this summer he must have sat up till dawn brightened over Westminster. There was a ball at the Embassy of her Turkish ally, and she chose the Ambassador as her partner (what would the Prophet have said?) and remembering all the private practice in the dining-room at old Balmoral, she danced Scotch reels to the skirling of bagpipes in the Waterloo Room.

The Princess Royal's marriage was fixed for the last week in January 1858. Already there had been a slight misunderstanding about the *venue*, but this the Queen had cleared up with the firmness, which, when occasion demanded, was peculiarly her own. It was the practice that Prussian Princes should be married in Berlin, and the suggestion had been made that this marriage should take place there. In such cases she did not argue with people; she told them and she told Lord Clarendon, her Foreign Minister: "Whatever may be the usual practice of Prussian Princes, it is not *every* day that one marries the eldest daughter of the Queen of England. The question therefore must be considered as settled and closed." Closed it was, and, instead, the Princess' future Court came to England for a three weeks' visit. Seventeen German Royalties were her guests for the festivities that preceded the wedding, and though she and the Prince Consort had set their hearts on the marriage, as linking together the Royal Houses of England and Prussia, the parting was agonising. The Princess and her father were devotedly attached to each other: she was the very reflection of his mind, sharing all his artistic and literary tastes and, in spite of her youth, affording him intellectual companionship to a degree the Queen had never done. No such ties bound mother and daughter, and indeed, as long as she had Albert by her, the Queen could not miss even a beloved daughter with a sense of desolation. Like her father, as her life soon proved, the Princess was incapable of naturalizing herself in the country which by blood was almost wholly hers, and to the end she remained an Englishwoman in Germany, even as he was a German in England.

One of the last photographs of Prince Albert and Queen
Victoria together, 1861.

The Prince of Wales (the future Edward VII) aged 9,
drawn by his mother with additions by SIR EDWIN
LANDSEER, one of her favourite artists.

VIII · FATHER AND SON

THERE NOW CAME DISAPPOINTMENTS in that domestic life which to the Emperor Napoleon was so fine an example for the Courts of Europe, and was to the Queen her private Empire on which the sun never set. Since the time when the heir to the throne was in the cradle, the education which should most nobly prepare him for his destiny had been his father's constant preoccupation. The Prince Consort had early defined the general end in view: it was such an upbringing as should render him as unlike as possible to his maternal great uncles, and the Queen stated the same in other terms when she said that her fervent prayer (and everybody else's) was "to see him resemble his angelic dearest Father in *every every* respect both in body and mind." At his parents' instance Stockmar had prepared two vast memoranda on the education of Princes, which in thoroughness left nothing to be desired. Indeed some of the Baron's precepts came perilously near to the obvious, for he was very emphatic that the Prince of Wales must "*unquestionably be trained*" in the creed of the Church of England, as if there were some thought of his being brought up as a Buddhist. He observed that science and philosophy were fraught with anti-Christian speculations, and it was a question whether the young Prince (then aged seven) should think these problems out for himself or be forewarned. That theological point was referred to Bishop Wilberforce of Oxford. The disquieting enigmas of adolescence would presently arise: on those Sir James Clark, the Prince's private physician, would be consulted. But it was time now for systematic mental education to begin, and so at the age of seven a tutor was found for Bertie, the Reverend Henry Birch, who fulfilled Stockmar's requirement of being "morally good, intelligent, well informed and experienced."

The principles on which this system of education was based were totally wrong. The Prince Consort from his earliest years had been a natural student, a boy eager to learn from books and enjoying the study of them. He deduced therefore that since Bertie (ex hypothesi) must grow up into his image, he must learn to love books. At present he had no taste for them, and must therefore be rigorously fed with them: appetite, in fact must be induced by overfeeding. Then Bertie developed a boyish *Schwärm* for his tutor, and here indeed was an opportunity: he might possibly have begun to take an interest in his lessons, because Mr Birch would be pleased. The Prince Consort took another view: he remembered his own affection for Herr Florschütz, a disordered unnatural fancy, and he dismissed Mr Birch. This was a miserable experience for the boy, who wrote him round-hand notes of lamentation, and left small presents under his pillow. The next tutor frankly told the Prince that books were being applied too thickly, but so un-German a sentiment was anathema, and two more tutors were engaged.

Bertie was bidden to keep a diary, but any freedom of record was checked because his father would read and criticise. He was bidden to write to Stockmar in "the firm, large and legible hand," which the Baron had laid down as being indispensable for Princes, and tell him what had been arousing his intelligent interest. So Bertie (aged nine) told Stockmar about the waxwork figures of Thugs whom he had seen at Papa's Great Exhibition – surely that would be safe – and how those thrilling folk made a fine art of murder. But Stockmar wrote back that England (over which Bertie would one day rule) was a Christian country, "where such

atrocious acts are not even dreamed of." All companionship with boys of
his own age was forbidden: at the most, two or three boys from Eton
came up to have tea at Windsor, but they were never left alone with him;
his father was always on guard and led the embarrassed conversation
into such channels as he would himself have loved at that age. There were
walking tours in which, under copious invigilation, other boys were
allowed to join: there was a tour abroad, with a sojourn at Bonn, of

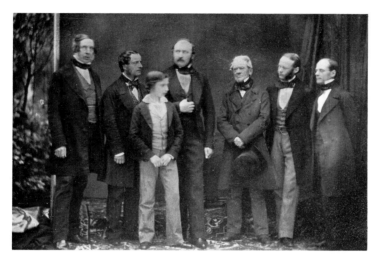

The young Prince, flanked by his taskmasters: LEFT TO
RIGHT, Col. Charles Phipps, F. W. Gibbs, Prince Albert,
Baron Stockmar, Dr E. Becker and Baron Ernst
Stockmar, 1857.

which the Prince Consort retained such studious and delightful memories, and here invigilation was multiplied, for Stockmar had warned the
parents of the danger of contaminating foreign habits, and four invigi-
lants took care of five small boys. But tutors' reports were monotonously
discouraging, and Bertie was not nearly so intelligent as his elder sister.

It seems strange that the Queen, remembering her "sad and lonely
childhood," should not have protested against so joyless a system, but
Albert must know best. The severance from boys of his own age was the
worst part of it, for Bertie was of a most companionable nature, much at
ease with others and sociable and well-mannered, yet it never struck her

that this natural geniality was an immense asset to a boy who would one day be king. Albert was stiff and aloof, so that was the ideal deportment. When Bertie was sixteen he was allowed to choose his own clothes, but that freedom was limited by a portentous memorandum from his mother, who, remembering how her Uncle, the last Prince of Wales, had taken his seat in the House of Lords in a black velvet coat covered with pink spangles, warned him against "*extravagance* or *slang*" in his attire, "because it would prove a want of respect and an offence against decency, leading – as it has often done before in others, to what is morally wrong" so there were sermons in coats. He was confirmed, and there his father took charge, and, like him, he was examined for an hour, in the presence of his parents, by the Archbishop of Canterbury and the Dean of Windsor. At the age of sixteen, when ordinary boys would have been at boarding-schools for six years or so, he first left his parents' roof, and was established at the White Lodge in Richmond Park with two tutors and a rota of equerries for his sole companions. These received exhaustive memoranda from the Queen and the Prince Consort as to their duties; and the Prince Consort, perhaps with remorseful memories of the soft cheese he had put in Cousin Linette's pockets and the frogs she had put in his bed, warned them to stamp out any tendency towards practical jokes. On his seventeenth birthday (1858) he was given the Order of the Garter and a fresh joint memorandum reminded him that life was composed of the duties set forth in the Church Catechism. Colonel Bruce was appointed as his Governor, and he must report himself to him whenever he left the house. Under his charge he spent three weeks in Rome, and, with the Governor in attendance, had an audience of the Pope, for if he went alone, so the Queen wrote to Uncle Leopold, His Holiness might announce that "Bertie had said God knows what." He was kept strictly at his books, and for relaxation visited the ruins of Roman buildings: in the evening eminent folk like Robert Browning and Frederick Leighton came to dinner. His Governor was instructed to take notes of his conversation and send them to his father with news of his mental progress. These reports were not favourable: Bertie attached undue importance to the pleasure of social intercourse, and his diary gave little satisfaction. He was not imbibing a hunger for art or a thirst for history, and the fact that he was the first Prince of Wales who had ever spoken to a Pope roused in him no reflections about the interesting spread of religious toleration.

He was a grievous disappointment, for with all this intensive culture he did not show the faintest promise of ever becoming the least like his father, and the Prince Consort cryptically lamented that he was neither fish nor flesh. He was stupid, he had no desire to learn, his temper was quick instead of blandly philosophical, and that sunny geniality which others found so attractive was only a symptom of a frivolous nature. But never was there any thought of modifying the curriculum of tutors and books and isolation. Bertie came home from Italy in June 1859, and was packed off to Edinburgh University for a couple of months until Oxford reassembled after that monstrous long vacation. Then followed three terms at Oxford, and to prevent contamination of his morals from dissolute undergraduates he lived with his Governor and tutor in a house called Frewin Hall, and the Professors of Chemistry, Modern Languages, Modern History and Ecclesiastical History came there to give him lectures. Smoking was forbidden, memoranda flew to and fro between Windsor and Oxford and the Prince Consort made surprise raids on the University to see that there was no slackness.

The Dominion of Canada had furnished a regiment in the Crimean War and the Queen had promised that the Prince of Wales should pay a visit there, when he was old enough. So, in the long vacation of 1860 he was allowed to make a tour through the Dominion and also go to Washington and New York. Wherever he went his geniality and personal charm asserted themselves. There had lately been a good deal of friction between the United States and England, and the Duke of Newcastle who accompanied him as Colonial Secretary reported that the ablest diplomacy could not have kindled such friendliness as the dunce had done. His father found it hard to credit such news, and there was certainly irony in his comment to Stockmar: "Bertie is generally pronounced the most perfect product of Nature." General Bruce was not so enthusiastic: he was afraid that the Prince was getting an undue sense of his own importance, which seemed to the Prince Consort much more likely, and so his father reminded him that the warmth of his welcome was entirely due to the fact that he was representing his mother. On his return he was sent straight back to Oxford, immured at Frewin Hall and still forbidden to smoke. After Christmas he was sent under similar limitations to Cambridge.

This strictness and supervision were farcical, they were also lamentable. Possibly the Prince Consort was subconsciously jealous of Bertie's reception, as of a young King, in the Dominion over which he would

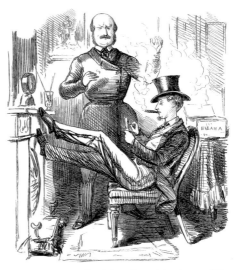

PUNCH cartoon emphasising the widening gulf between
Prince Albert and his son.

some day reign and in the United States. What splendour of Empire awaited this indolent unscholarly son of his, who at Oxford and Cambridge was rebelling against the restrictions which to himself would have been a service of perfect freedom: for the Prince Consort had ordained for him a life which at Bertie's age he would have considered an ideal existence. No late hours, no distractions, no pretty girls, but a bevy, a queue of professors waiting to instruct him, and unlimited opportunities for study!

In 1860 the Queen's second daughter, Princess Alice, was betrothed to Prince Louis of Hesse, which, as strengthening the family ties between England and Germany, was looked upon both by the Queen and the Prince Consort as highly satisfactory.

The year 1861 opened with every prospect of prosperity and domestic happiness. The death of the King of Prussia who had been insane since 1857, could not be considered as anything but a deliverance, and on the accession of his brother Prince William, who had been acting as Regent, Prince Frederick became Crown Prince. There were glad anniversaries to follow, first that of Vicky's wedding-day. Then came the thrice-blessed twenty-first anniversary of the Queen's own marriage. It filled her heart

Lithograph of Princess Alice, from a portrait by
WINTERHALTER.

with gratitude and love: it had brought "to the *world* at *large* such incalculable blessings," and as regards herself, "*Very* few can say with me that their husband at the end of twenty-one years is *not* only full of the friendship, kindness and affection which a truly happy marriage brings with it, but the same tender love of the *very first days of our marriage*."

And then there was Berties marriage to think about. Three years ago, while he was only sixteen, Uncle Leopold had drawn up a list of seven eligible Princesses of whom six were German (and were currently reported to be very assiduous in learning English). The seventh, fifth on Uncle Leopold's list, was Princess Alexandra, daughter of Prince Christian of Schleswig-Holstein-Sonderburg-Glucksburg: his wife Princess Louise of Hesse-Cassel was heiress to the Danish throne. The Prince

Consort made enquiries about this young lady from his daughter at Berlin, who gave the most enthusiastic report of her. This carried weight and the Prince promoted her to the top of Uncle Leopold's list. For reasons which would appeal to any very conscientious father, he thought that the sooner Bertie married the better, and it was planned that during that scandalously lengthy long vacation at Cambridge, he should be given a glimpse of No. 1.

Victoria's drawing of her younger child Princess
Beatrice with her grand-daughter Charlotte of Prussia,
1861.

Then fell the first blow of the year that was to prove so tragic. Immediately after his marriage Albert had done away with that unhappy estrangement which existed between the Queen and her mother, and now for over twenty years they had been on most affectionate terms. The Duchess of Kent had Frogmore in Windsor Park for her country residence, and Clarence House in London, and when the Court was at Balmoral she was close by at Abergeldie. She was now in her seventy-fifth year, still rather foreign in speech, a cheerful and lively old lady, finding the evening of life a very serene and agreeable hour, devoted to her grandchildren and above all to Albert. She was seriously ill for only one day and died on March 16, 1861. The Queen was bewildered with grief,

The Duchess of Kent, Victoria's mother, photographed
in 1856, five years before her death.

yet even in the first shock of this close bereavement, the most intimate she had ever known, death, the mystery and silence of it, had the strange fascination for her which she felt while quite a child, and she poured out to her diary and to Uncle Leopold a flood of details and emotions. Everything connected with her mother became "dearly and passionately loved," and Frogmore must be kept exactly as she left it. Her presence still dwelt there, and daily the Queen went there to realize the blank in her life.

The death bed of the Prince Consort. Photograph of the
Blue Room, Windsor Castle, where he died on 14
December, 1861.

Life moved forward again: there was a succession of Royal visitors, and the Queen and the Prince Consort went over to Ireland in August to see the Prince of Wales who, though still under the eye of General Bruce, had been allowed to learn the duties of a subaltern in the Grenadier Guards, of which he was a Colonel, at the Curragh Camp. His father was not pleased with him or the other officers: they were not earnest enough about their profession. Bertie had better spend the remainder of that ludicrously long Cambridge vacation in Germany, where he would learn what keen fellows young German officers were. He had now been told about the matrimonial plans devised for him, and it was arranged that he should, while abroad, meet Princess Alexandra, now first on the list. So off he went from this slack Curragh Camp, and having seen No. 1, expressed no wish to see the six other eligibles, who, presumably, shut up their English grammars and dictionaries.

The Court went to Balmoral. There was an unusual number of "Great Expeditions" made incognito. Sometimes their identity was suspected, and once they actually were discovered, and a band saluted them, and the "fat old landlady of the inn where they were lodging put on a black satin dress with white ribbons and orange flowers." A Highland gillie John Brown was now her factotum: he waited at table, he led her pony, and, as she wrote to Uncle Leopold, "he combined the offices of groom, footman, page and maid, I might almost say, as he is so handy about cloaks and shawls."

The Prince Consort always found the English autumn trying: he was sleeping badly, but the Queen thought him better than he usually was at this time of the year. Towards the end of the month he got a chill inspecting the new buildings of the Military College at Sandhurst, and was rather rheumatic. There seemed no cause for anxiety, and a few days later he went down to Cambridge where the Prince of Wales was keeping his term.

On the morning of December 1 the Prince Consort was sent to bed, but moved on to his sofa in the afternoon: there was restlessness, sleeplessness and loss of appetite, but neither the Queen nor the doctors were anxious. Sir James Clark diagnosed "a feverish sort of influenza" and at the end of the first week of December he seemed better. Then Dr. Jenner was called in and diagnosed typhoid. Reckoning from the day when the Prince first felt ill, after his visit to Sandhurst, he was now in the third week of the attack and improvement might be looked for, as his strength kept up and there were no unfavourable symptoms. The Queen continued to write quite cheerfully to Uncle Leopold, and it would seem that the doctors shared her views for the Prince of Wales was not sent for as must have been done if there was any real cause for alarm. Then came a sudden relapse, a telegram was sent to Cambridge, but when the Prince arrived it is doubtful whether his father knew him. He died on the night of December 14, 1861.

The mourning Queen and her daughter, Princess Alice,
photographed by her son, Prince Alfred, Windsor 1862.

Detail from a plate commemorating the life and
achievements of the Prince Consort.

IX · CLINGING TO GRIEF

THE WHOLE FABRIC of the Queen's domestic happiness was shattered. Albert had often spoken to her of the shortness of life, but she had felt "with instinctive certainty" that it would be granted to them to grow old together. In the darkness she clung, curiously unreticent, to the simple faith from which she had never wavered. To one Minister she wrote: "The things of this world are of no interest to the Queen . . . for her thoughts are fixed above." To another that she had only "one consolation – to rejoin *him* again, never to part," and to Uncle Leopold that this parting "must be for *his* good, his happiness . . . His great soul is *now only* enjoying that for which it *was* worthy. And I will not envy him – only pray that *mine* may be perfected by it, and fit to be with him *eternally* for which blessed moment I earnestly long . . . He seems so *near* to me, so quite my own now . . ."

From that conviction – the sense of his living presence, and of the sure reunion – sprang an inevitable resolution. In life he had been "her Angel and Master," his mind, known to her and her alone, had been the incarnation of a wisdom almost divine and by that and that alone she would shape her days.

Straight from the exuberant noonday of her life, and the vivid vitality of her early middle-age, she passed without pause into a long-drawn and melancholy evening. In that seclusion and eclipse she devoted herself to fulfilling the secret testament of Albert's wishes and plans known to herself alone, both in the public affairs of State and in the private direction of her family. Yet, oddly enough, the whole conduct of her life in its complete withdrawal from the functions which are no small part of

Wedding photograph of the Prince of Wales and Alexandra, grouped around the marble bust of the deceased Albert.

monarchical duties, must surely have been in flat opposition to what Albert himself would have wished. She allowed the shrinking from all public contacts, natural to the first weeks or even months of mourning, wholly to obsess her. Long ago she had written, "How one *loves* to cling to one's grief," and she clung to it till it became to her a habit of morbid luxury, and out of it grew her hypochondriacal conviction that the state of her health would not permit her to do anything she found disagreeable. Her work was vastly increased by her determination to adhere to Albert's rule of reading and criticising every document that required her signature, however trivial it might be or however technical, and she clung to the prerogatives of the Crown with all her pertinacity.

In the summer of 1862 came the marriage, already arranged and approved by the Prince Consort, of Princess Alice and Prince Louis of Hesse. The joyless and almost clandestine ceremony was performed in the drawing-room at Osborne. Then the more important matrimonial project for the Prince of Wales must be proceeded with. His mother had never yet seen Princess Alexandra, but she was first on the list of eligibles, and so in the strictest privacy the Queen went to stay with Uncle Leopold at Brussels, to meet her and her parents. Again her dominating thought was that it was "a terrible moment" for her to speak to them about the marriage without Albert's support. The young girl's beauty and charm made a most favourable impression, but still that determined joylessness prevailed and the Queen feared that the Princess would be entering a very sad house. Bertie could now be sent for to speak for himself, and the Queen went on to Coburg to visit the scenes that were now a shrine to her. News came that he had proposed and been accepted, and the Queen herself wrote the communication to the English press which announced the betrothal, stating that "it was based entirely upon mutual affection and the personal merits of the Princess, and was in no way connected with political considerations." She added, sealing it with final authority, that "The revered Prince Consort whose sole object was the education and welfare of his children had been long convinced that this was a most desirable marriage."

The wedding was celebrated on March 10, 1863 at St George's Chapel, Windsor, for the Queen absolutely refused to have it at Westminster Abbey, since she would have had to make a public appearance, and, though a widow of fifteen months, she would not put off her crape for a single day. She took no part in the function, only watching it from a gallery in the Chapel.

The Queen's very full account of the day, as given in her diary, is a key to the long seclusion that followed. To the nation the marriage of the heir to the throne was naturally an event for flags and peals of bells, but to his mother every incident, every moment of it kindled some spark of heartbreaking memory which she cherished and blew into flame. And how she suffered while the ceremony was going on to think that the "guardian angel of the family" was not there; and how the departure of

EPISODE DURING A BRIEF VISIT TO LONDON.

AUGUST PERSONAGE: "What is that large empty building there?"
FOOTMAN: "Please, your Majesty, that's Buckingham Palace."

the young married couple for their honeymoon recalled "*our* driving away twenty-three years ago *to* Windsor." Not a gleam of joy at her son's marriage illumined her desolation, not a gleam of thankfulness for her own twenty-one years of domestic happiness, or that eight of her children were gathered round her, and that there was good news of Alfred who was recovering from typhoid in Malta. By that cruel, irresistible alchemy of hypochondria in this difficult period of a woman's life, she transmuted motherly joy into the emptiness of widowhood, and re-fashioned flags and banners into instruments for her own self-torture.

Previously to her husband's death she had mainly been in London while Parliament was sitting, as was only right for a Sovereign who insisted on being consulted by her Ministers on every point that might arise, but from now onwards she certainly did not on the average spend a week of the year in town. For four months at the outside she was at Windsor, the remainder she passed at her two sequestered country homes which Albert had created. For some weeks in May and June

Cartoon comment on the Queen's long seclusion after
Albert's death.

during the session she was always at Balmoral, and though a Ministerial crisis might threaten she would make the greatest difficulty about postponing her journey there even by a day or two or hastening her return: often she refused altogether. Strange, indeed, was the contrast between this indifference to her duties and the conscientiousness which had forbade her to spend more than a couple of days of honeymoon after her marriage at Windsor. Now nothing would induce her to be on the spot, though, in the remote wilds of the Highlands, feeding her grief, she worked at State business with unremitting industry. For that, when presently a general feeling arose that she had much better abdicate in favour of her son, she was never given due credit. She was a slave to such duties as she could perform unseen and absent.

Unfortunately this seclusion in which she cherished the sense of her loss, made a forcing-house for its perpetuation, and her morbid self-pity flourished side by side with hypochondriacal fears for her health. She was in a state of nervous instability in which her own comfort, as always happens in such cases, was a constant preoccupation. She thought that Princess Alice and her husband and her baby ought to make their home with her instead of going back to their own home at Darmstadt. Then she fixed on her next unmarried daughter Princess Helena. She did not intend, she wrote to Uncle Leopold, that the Princess should marry for two or three years yet, but when she did, the Queen "could *not* give her up without *sinking* under the *weight* of my desolation." She would therefore look out for a "young sensible Prince . . . who can during MY lifetime make my house his principal home." A good character with sufficient means to support her daughter in case of her own death was all she asked for. Again it seemed a cruel piece of selfishness that her valued Lady-in-waiting, Lady Augusta Bruce, had at the age of forty-one "most unnecessarily decided to marry (!!) that certainly most distinguished and excellent man Dr Stanley!! . . . It has been my *greatest sorrow* and trial since my misfortune! *I* thought she *never* would leave *me*!" She fondled her ailments: she referred her Uncle to her doctors in order that they should tell him "how very important it is that I should have *no* excitement, *no* agitation, IF I am to live on." She believed that she would die sooner than any of them thought: "for myself this would be the *greatest*

greatest blessing: but for the poor children I feel a *few* more years would be desirable, and for the country, I *own*, it alarms me still more." For Bertie would be King, and one of the main clauses in her melancholy creed was his unfitness. Between the work that was a sacred duty to her, and, for relaxation, this incessant dwelling on herself, it says much for the essential soundness of her constitution that these years of seclusion did not wreck her health.

Princess Helena, in mourning dress. Lithograph after a painting by WINTERHALTER, done before her marriage.

In 1863 trouble in Europe over the Duchies of Schleswig-Holstein brought discord into the Queen's private life. The three claimants to the Duchies were Prussia, Denmark and Duke Frederick of Schleswig-Holstein-Sonderburg-Augustenburg. The Crown Prince and Princess of Prussia came to stay at Windsor in December, and though the Queen had always believed that the consanguinity of high Royal personages conduced to harmony between their countries, it was now apparent that disagreements between countries conduced to painful discord between the consanguine. The Queen indeed found herself the only true Prussian present, for Fritz and Vicky, who both detested Bismarck and all his works, were upholders of Duke Frederick, while Bertie and Alix were both of them, now that war was imminent, violently pro-Denmark. It was all so painful (and it was not good for Alix to be excited just now) that the Queen exercised her rights as a hostess and said she hoped she would not hear the words Schleswig-Holstein again . . . But plenary forgiveness was granted to the Danes when on January 8, 1864 the Princess of Wales gave birth to a son. The birth was premature by two months, and the Queen hurried from Osborne to Frogmore to be with

Prince Christian of Schleswig-Holstein, husband of
Princess Helena, 1866.

her daughter-in-law. "Albert" must be the baby's first name: and the Queen took the opportunity to impress on the Prince that when he came to the Throne he must be known as King Albert Edward. It would be monstrous to drop his father's name, and Albert alone would not do, "as there can be only *one* ALBERT." The baby, she privately thought was "a poor little bit of a thing," but it stood in the direct succession, and London must not be deprived of "the honour and gratification" of its being christened there. The private chapel of Buckingham Palace would be the least public place, and though it would be a great trial she, D.V., would hold the baby herself and present it to the Archbishop of Canterbury.

By December the Duchies were in the hands of Prussia and Austria; Duke Frederick had been deprived of his estates and his younger brother, Prince Christian, had been obliged to give up his commission in the Prussian Army. The Queen already had Prince Christian in her mind as a possible husband for her third daughter Princess Helena, for, having no country of his own, he would naturally live in England, and so she would not be parted from her daughter. He had not, it is true, much independent means, but Parliament would no doubt help. Otherwise he was most suitable: Duke Ernest thought highly of him, and the Crown Princess to whom she had applied early in the year gave him an excellent character. He was amusing when he chose, he spoke English and was "the best creature in the world." So when the Queen went to Coburg again in August to unveil a further statue of the Prince Consort, she took Princess Helena with her, and her brother-in-law invited Prince Christian, and the betrothal took place.

The Queen returned to Balmoral, and there on October 15 the news of Lord Palmerston's serious illness reached her. It was the twenty-sixth anniversary of her own betrothal: that, and the fear that in case of his death she might have to leave for Windsor a few days earlier than she had intended were her first thoughts. He died three days afterwards, and with almost vindictive honesty, she made no pretence to forgive the past. "I never liked him," she wrote to her Uncle, "or could even the least respect him, nor could I forget his conduct on certain occasions to my Angel." He was eighty, he had been a Minister of the Crown with short intermissions for fifty-eight years, but she could say no more for this lifetime of service than that he had many valuable qualities though many bad ones . . . Poor Lord Palmerston, "*alias* Pilgerstein." Before the year was out came yet another death, that of Uncle Leopold on December 10. She felt his loss but with no sense of despair. She had known him from the days of her babyhood, he had been the chief contriver of her blissful marriage, he was wrapped up with the past and in the Mausoleum his spirit seemed strangely to mingle with Albert's. But her sense of the past was really filled by one memory only.

Since 1861 the Queen had absolutely ignored the hitherto unbroken tradition of the Sovereign opening Parliament in person, and when in

1864 her Ministers had tried to induce her to resume it, she said it "was totally out of the question" by reason of the "moral shocks" and fatigue it would entail and there was the end of it. But the resentment of the nation against her continued invisibility was getting serious and there was an additional reason why she should appear in person at the opening of the session in 1866, namely that she intended to ask Parliament for two more grants for her children, a dowry of £30,000 with an annuity of £6000 for Princess Helena on her approaching marriage, and an annuity of £15,000 for Prince Alfred on his coming of age. If once more she absented herself there was a horrid chance of her Commons refusing supplies, and she steeled herself to the effort.

The settling of the date for the function produced endless difficulties. And then she felt she must once for all express to Lord Russell the agony she was going through: "The Queen must say that she does feel *very bitterly* the want of feeling of those who *ask* the Queen to go to open Parliament. That the public should wish to see her she fully understands, and has *no* wish to prevent – quite the contrary: but why this wish should be of so *unreasonable* and unfeeling a nature as to *long* to *witness* the spectacle of a poor widow, nervous and shrinking, dragged in *deep mourning* ALONE *in* STATE as a *Show* where she used to go supported by her husband to be gazed at, without delicacy of feeling, is a thing *she cannot* understand, and she never could wish her bitterest foe to be exposed to!"

In spite of the Queen's passionate denunciation of those who were unfeeling enough to make her open Parliament, the rigidity of her seclusion began to melt a little. She reviewed troops at Aldershot, she attended the wedding of her beloved cousin Mary of Cambridge to the Duke of Teck, son by a morganatic marriage of Duke Alexander of Würtemberg, and first cousin of the Queen on her mother's side. She held a Drawing Room at Buckingham Palace, though nothing would induce her not to flee to Balmoral exactly when a Ministerial crisis occurred over the Reform Bill in June. While she was there the Government was defeated and Lord Russell resigned. She was extremely angry with him, for she had particularly desired him to hold on while she was away, and she refused to accept his resignation. On coming back to Windsor she sent for Lord Derby who took office, with Disraeli as Chancellor of the Exchequer. She wondered at her own firmness, still immensely pitying herself, but she no longer felt that her people wished to look at her as a "Show." On the contrary there was "something peculiar and touching in the joy and even emotion with which they greeted their poor widowed Queen," and that was a great change. Again in February 1867, she opened Parliament without any nervous crisis. Lord Derby had but to tell her that her presence would give moral support to her Government and she consented at once, though with the stipulation that it must be "clearly understood that she is *not* expected to do it as a *matter* of course, year after year."

The ebbed tide had certainly begun to flow again, slowly but perceptibly, and she began to dwell on the vanished years less with personal desolation than with a treasuring pride that they were hers and with the desire that all the world should know her Angel as he was. Her habit of thought reversed itself and, instead of wailing over the irrevocable, she unsealed from it a spring of renewed vitality. General Grey, once the Prince Consort's Secretary and now her own, had already brought out, under the Queen's supervision, a history of his early years, and now she asked Mr Theodore Martin to write his whole life on a much larger scale. The real truth and nothing but the truth, as she knew it, must be told: the Prince must be shewn, full length, as he was to her. She supplied the mass of his private papers on which these five substantial volumes were based, and read and criticised every chapter as it was written. For herself, she added supplementary side-lights of her own composition, by making with Sir Arthur Helps's assistance, a volume of extracts from her diary entitled "Leaves from a Journal of our Life in the Highlands from 1848 to 1861." It was privately published in 1867, and at Sir Arthur's promptings given to the public next year, with elaborate biographical notes by the Queen about the gillies, keepers and personal attendants who figure so constantly in its pages. It was out and away the best seller of the year, and there is nothing to wonder at in that, for it consisted entirely of those domestic trivialities, into which, in the lives of the eminent, the public loves to be admitted. Simplicity was the keynote of its contents and its style: it dealt with picnics and dogs and sunsets, with teas on the hillside, and the difficulty of making water boil out of doors, with Albert stalking

Colour print commemorating Queen Victoria's Jubilee
with vignettes of the marriages of two of her children.

Unveiling the memorial statue of Albert at Coburg. 26th
August, 1865. Watercolour by G. H. Thomas.

Queen Victoria visiting the Royal Mausoleum at Frogmore. Watercolour by H. Brewer.

JUNE 21ST 1887

Jubilee banquet at Buckingham Palace, 21 June, 1887.
Watercolour by R. T. PRITCHETT.

Queen Victoria with John Brown,
painting by C. B. Barber.

Map illustrating the extent of the British Empire in 1886.
1887 Jubilee, Queen Victoria and her children.

Colour print of Queen Victoria published by THE TIMES
to commemorate the 1897 Jubilee.

Memorial painting of Queen Victoria
by Henry Campotosto.

a stag and Vicky sitting down on a wasps' nest. As for the style, which Sir Arthur Helps thought too colloquial, it was an admirable vehicle for what it conveyed, and the Queen was right to defend it, for: "It was the simplicity of the style and the absence of all appearance of writing for effect which had given the book such immense and undeserved success."

There were occasional serious relapses in this welcome process of revitalization, in which, for one whose nerves were shattered and who thought herself on the verge of a complete breakdown, she fought with amazing vigour in defence of her seclusion. One such occurred at the time of the International Exhibition in Paris in 1867. The Emperor Napoleon was making a tremendous occasion of this, and among his guests for the Prize-giving Day were to be Tsar Alexander II of Russia, the Emperor of Austria, the Sultan of Turkey, the Khedive Ismail of Egypt, and the Prince of Wales who was President of the Royal Commission for the English section: he had also asked the Pope who declined.

Some of these crowned heads planned to cross from France to England after the Exhibition and it was most important that England should make a suitable gesture. But would the Queen make it? It seemed very doubtful, for she worked herself up into a nervous crisis over the idea of her having to entertain Royal guests. The worst of it was that Royal personages were coming to England whether she liked it or not, for the Sultan Abdul Aziz and the Khedive Ismail had already signified their intention of doing so. Never before, so the Prime Minister pointed out, had a Sultan visited London: English influence just now was paramount at Constantinople, it was most important to maintain it, and after the magnificent reception Napoleon would have given him in Paris, it would be disastrous if he was welcomed less royally here. The Queen replied that she would give him lodging at Buckingham Palace, but she would not put forward her return from Balmoral by a single day on his account: rest and quiet were essential for her. Moreover since the Sultan's visit was a matter of political importance, the Government ought to bear part of the expense of his entertainment. But when the date of the Sultan's visit was settled, she found she would naturally be at Osborne, and thought that a Naval Review would interest him. She would go out on the *Victoria and Albert*, unless the weather was bad, and receive him.

The Queen investing Abdul Aziz, Sultan of Turkey, with
the Order of the Garter, 1867.

Otherwise he might pay her a morning call at Osborne. What did Lord Derby think of that?

Lord Derby thought very poorly of it. According to the proposed dates the Sultan would have been languishing at Buckingham Palace for five days before the Naval Review without seeing her at all. Could she not stop at Windsor for three days before she went to Osborne, so as to be there when the Sultan arrived, and either welcome him at Buckingham Palace – ten minutes would be sufficient – or let him come to lunch with her at Windsor? Her Government thought it so important that they would sign a Minute of the Cabinet about it. At that her indignation at this interference with her private plans became hysterical. Surely if the Sultan knew how inconvenient it was to put off her departure for Osborne he would come a day earlier! She longed for the time when she could go to that world "where the wicked cease from troubling and the weary are at rest." She sent Dr. Jenner to Lord Derby to tell him what the real state of her nerves was. She would not be dictated to or teased by public clamour into doing "what she *physically* CANNOT." But she yielded.

Owing to the exertions of the Prince of Wales this extremely important visit went off very well. He met the Sultan at Dover, he took him down to lunch with his mother next day at Windsor and kept him gorged with entertainments and receptions till the day of the Naval Review. Then there was the question of what Order he should receive, and the Prince convinced her that to offer any Order except the Garter to a reigning Sovereign, be he Christian or Moslem, would be nothing less than an insult; his predecessor had been given it after the Crimean War, and the Sultan had set his heart on it. So the Queen invested him with it when he came on board the *Victoria and Albert* at the Naval Review. Evidently she rather enjoyed the day, and noted humorous incidents in her Journal: how Ismail, who accompanied the Sultan, had very short legs, and had to sit on the extreme edge of his chair in order to get his feet on the ground: how the Sultan, being a poor sailor, made frequent retirements below, and thus did not see much of the Review. But he was enchanted with his visit and his decoration, and thanks to the Prince, left England in a very good temper.

Benjamin Disraeli, one of the Queen's favourite Prime
Ministers, wreathed in primroses.

Cartoon of Gladstone, 1869, by C. PELLEGRINI.

X · DISRAELI AMUSES

UNFORTUNATELY THE QUEEN showed no signs of revising her low opinion of her eldest son's abilities and trustworthiness, and in default of any regular employment he had to devote his exuberant energies to amusing himself. It was her adherence to this conjugal tradition, mixed with a personal, subconsciously jealous unwillingness that he should take her place in any way, that made her so reluctant, in the spring of 1868, to let him visit Ireland as her representative, shewing that she took an interest in that perturbed portion of her dominions. The country was riddled with Fenianism, but the Prince and his wife were as scornful of personal risks as she was herself and she opposed the visit for ridiculous reasons. She had a Viceroy there already: he represented her, and the question of precedence between them would be a very difficult problem. The programme included a visit to the Punchestown races: that would never do. He attended far too many race-meetings as it was. Had it not been for the advocacy of her new Prime Minister Mr. Disraeli, who had succeeded Lord Derby on his retirement earlier in the year, she would probably not have permitted the visit at all. But Mr. Disraeli had already begun to establish himself with her, and, by careful observation, to learn how to manage her, she consented to the visit.

Disraeli had made a good beginning. This year he was Prime Minister for only ten months but the flute was seldom out of his mouth. Twice before, when he had been Chancellor of the Exchequer, she had found his despatches far more entertaining than the cut and dried communications of other Ministers, and he made them more seductive yet with deft adoring touches. She was his gracious Mistress: he compared the speakers of the Opposition "to a company, a *troupe*, like one of those bands of minstrels one encounters in the sauntering of a summer street . . . but with visages not so fair and radiant as the countenances of your Majesty's subjects at Balmoral." He never hinted that her long absences in her northern home were highly inconvenient: he only earnestly hoped "that the bright air of Balmoral, and your Majesty's serene life have at the same time strengthened and tranquillised a nervous system very sensitive and too much tried." How different was this comprehending sympathy from the odious cruelty of the Press. She sent him a box of spring flowers from Osborne and he told her that: "None of the decorations on which he sometimes has to take your Majesty's pleasure were half so fair."

Then he was indefatigable in examining the merits of candidates for high ecclesiastical appointments, and though such subjects were new to him, he shewed great discernment, recommending, for instance, Dr. McNeile for the Deanery of Ripon on account of his "eloquent, learned and commanding advocacy of the Royal supremacy." He stayed at Balmoral in the autumn as Minister in attendance, and the Queen found him extremely agreeable and original, and they had great talks about preferment in the Church. She loaded him with gifts before he left: there were two volumes of views of Balmoral, a box full of family photographs, a full-length portrait of the Prince Consort, and a Scotch shawl for Mrs. Disraeli with a gracious message that the Queen hoped she would find it warm in the cold weather. His letter of thanks was most adroit: "though absent he will be able to live, as it were, in your Majesty's favourite scenes": the portrait was of that gifted being on whom his memory could not dwell without emotion, and nothing could more deeply gratify him than the Queen's recollection of his wife. Then this romantic partnership came temporarily to an end, for the Government was heavily defeated at the General Election in November, and the Queen sent for Mr. Gladstone who became her Prime Minister for the first time.

But Disraeli was well content with his achievements of the last ten months. Politically, his period of office had been of the most barren, but he had laid the foundation of such relations to the Queen as no Prime Minister, not even Melbourne, the idol of her girlish adoration, had ever enjoyed yet. He betook himself to the writing of his romance, *Lothair*, and read pieces of it to the newly created Viscountess Beaconsfield who, in that severe winter, was keeping warm in her Scotch shawl.

Throughout the first year of Gladstone's first Administration, there had been endless points of disagreement – some very insignificant – between him and the Queen, which promised an abundant fructification. The Queen was beginning not to like him personally, and she was always prone to let her personal feelings cloud her judgment. Though the Prime Minister's manner to her was most deferential, she did not like to be told that her public appearances were indispensable in maintaining the loyalty and devotion of her subjects. Her long and constant periods of retreat at Osborne and Balmoral not only occasioning the greatest inconvenience to her Ministers but dislocation in critical times of the machinery of the State were, in his opinion, totally unwarranted on the score of her health, and her fancied incapacity, backed up by the feeble-minded Jenner, had no real existence. Such dissonances, faintly but unmistakably audible in this first year of Gladstone's ministry, were not likely to be resolved into harmony.

At this time, as elsewhere in Europe, a wave of republicanism, with Sir Charles Dilke as its chief spokesman, was sweeping through the country fed largely by the Queen's repeated requests to Parliament for money for her numerous children as they came of age or married, and by her reluctance to appear at public State functions. Believing that these republican agitations all over England threatened the stability of the Monarchy, Gladstone repeatedly tried to coax the Queen out of her seclusion. But the Queen was adamant. Then Providence intervened. The Prince of Wales after celebrating his birthday in November fell ill of typhoid fever, and for the first fortnight of December he lay between life and death. One day the bulletins held out hope: on the next there was a relapse, and all that could be said was that he was still alive. Instantly the squalls of republicanism were stilled, the Queen and her heir ceased to exist as such and became a mother – any mother – watching by the bed of her son. To her the suspense was doubly dreadful, for each day brought nearer the anniversary of December 14 when ten years before the Prince Consort died of that same deadly fever and she felt almost sure that that dread day would rob her also of her son. Instead he took a decided turn for the better, and the country rejoiced over his convalescence with the same sincerity as it had followed his illness. The situation remained precisely the same as before with a withdrawn and expensive Queen and a hedonistic and expensive heir, but that deep-rooted sentimentalism, characteristic of the English, decided that the slate was wiped clean by all that they had been through. When next in the House of Commons Sir Charles Dilke proposed an audit into the Queen's accounts he found himself in a minority of four to nearly three hundred. The Prince's illness had literally given its death-blow to republicanism.

The Queen's nervous malaise and the natural causes of it were yielding before her increased vitality. Early in 1873 she went to see the lately-widowed Empress Eugénie at Chislehurst, she stayed at Buckingham Palace for a night, she drove down to the East End of London and opened the Victoria Park, and in June the Shah of Persia came to England and stayed for a fortnight at Buckingham Palace. His visit was of high political significance, for Russia's expansions in Asia rendered it very desirable that Anglo-Persian relations should be cordial: while amity between Russia and England, it was hoped, would be warmed up by the engagement of Prince Alfred, Duke of Edinburgh, to the Grand Duchess Marie, only daughter of Tsar Alexander II and sister to the Tsarevitch. By a clever plan the Tsarevitch and his wife, sister of the Princess of Wales, were staying with the Prince at Marlborough House while the Shah was at Buckingham Palace; Russia and Persia were thus being welcomed in England simultaneously. The very day after the Shah's arrival, June 20, the anniversary of the Queen's accession, she received him in full state at Windsor, and the gusto of her account in her Journal once more proved how thoroughly she enjoyed State functions when she could screw herself up to them. She invested him with the Garter and kissed him. In return he invested her with two Orders, one of which he had invented just before he left Persia, and her cap was in danger of coming off, but the Grand Vizier, Princess Christian and Princess Louise came to its rescue. They sat down to lunch to the skirl of Highland pipers, and the Shah told her that he had caused her "Leaves from the Journal of a Life in the

The Shah of Persia, with the Prince and Princess of
Wales, during his visit to England in 1873.

Highlands" to be translated into Persian and that he had read it. He lunched on fruit and quantities of iced water, and then went to have a rest attended by his Pipe-bearer and Cup-bearer. When he appeared again he had taken off his diamond aigrette and put on his spectacles. Not a word of wailing was there now about the impossibility of entertaining Royalty without the support of the Prince Consort: on another day she took him to a Military Review, and on their third meeting, they exchanged photographs and he was taken to the Mausoleum . . . How about Mr Gladstone's complaints that she would not perform the decorative functions of a Monarch?

In the General Elections of 1874, the Conservatives were returned

The Queen receiving the Shah of Persia at Windsor
Castle in 1873.

with a substantial majority. Disraeli was sent for and became Prime Minister for the second time. To the Queen the change was like passing, after a most uncomfortable voyage over choppy seas, into a sheltered harbour festooned with bunting and mottoes. Her relief from the rolling and pitching was so great that her parting from Gladstone was unnaturally cordial, and it might be augured that she would find it difficult to keep that up if ever in the future she would have to say "Hail" to him again instead of "Farewell."

Disraeli's success in this troubadour style was instantly apparent. Never before (except in those few months when he was feeling his way) had she worked with so amusing a Prime Minister, and, with her returning strength and her reaction from harangues, her appetite for amusement had come back to her. He turned his prodigious sense of the romantic and of the picturesque on to her, as if it had been an arc-light, and she saw herself illuminated in that carefully-adjusted beam. Mr. Disraeli amused her, and how, after Mr. Gladstone, she liked being amused!

It was Disraeli who persuaded the Queen to consent to the Prince of Wales making a tour of India and he left England in September 1875.

The thought of India continued to "rouse vibrations" in the minds of the Queen and her Prime Minister after H.M.S. *Serapis* had left European shores. Passing through the Red Sea the Prince wrote to Lord Granville about the Suez Canal: "It is certainly an astounding work, and it is an extraordinary pity that it was not made by an English Company and kept in our hands, because as it is our highway to India, we should [in case of trouble there] be obliged to take it – by force of arms if necessary." It was Palmerston who had missed that chance and now it was for Disraeli, his great admirer, to rectify it. Luck favoured him: Turkey was nearly bankrupt and the Khedive Ismail owing to his monstrous extravagance more than bankrupt, and the opportunity occurred of purchasing his shares in the Canal. The price was £4,000,000, and the compatriot House of Rothschild furnished the cash within ten days. Disraeli announced the purchase to the Queen in his best style as if the Canal was her private property like Osborne or Balmoral: "It is just settled; you have it, Madam!" The importance of the Suez Canal as regards India had

Scene during the Prince of Wales' visit to Jaipur, India in
1875.

never entered her head before, but this personal present delighted her, as
he knew it would.

The success of the tour caused a project which had long been in the
Queen's mind to revive again. After the Indian Mutiny there had been a
suggestion that she should add to her "style" Empress of India, and again
in 1873 she had privately put the question before Gladstone's India
Office, but nothing had come of it. Secretly, she still hankered after it, and
now that Bertie, as her representative, was making himself so popular,
here was an admirable opportunity to take it up again, and she thought it
would give the greatest satisfaction in India. She notified her wish to
Disraeli and Lord Salisbury, neither of whom, though acquiescing, was
at all enthusiastic.

In Parliament there was violent opposition which "shocked and
surprised" the Queen, and called from her volleys of uncompromising
epithets. Disraeli himself described the piloting of the Bill conferring her
new title through the House as an exposure of weeks to a fiery furnace,

but the Queen sent him a portrait of herself which he assured her would "animate and sustain him in many cares and troubles."

One of these troubles was a letter from the Prince, furious at not having been told about the business, he said that India, instead of being gratified, was perfectly indifferent to the honour done to her teeming millions. But the Bill went through, and the fiery furnace subsided, and Disraeli took the portrait down to Hughenden, for he did not want to be parted from it while he was in London. But he felt old and tired, and "V.R. and I" more delighted with him than ever, created him Earl of Beaconsfield when the Session was over, and, as Prime Minister still, he directed the ship from the less stormswept bridge of the House of Lords.

PUNCH's view of Victoria's ennoblement of her Prime Minister, Benjamin Disraeli.

23 July, 1885. Wedding group of Princess Beatrice and
Prince Henry of Battenberg at Osborne.

Queen Victoria's watercolour of her favourite Indian
servant, Abdul Karim.

XI · EMPIRE BUILDING

THE NEXT THREE YEARS saw the outbreak of renewed conflict in the Balkans and in 1877, when Russia declared war on Turkey, the Mediterranean Fleet was ordered to Constantinople. The effect of this continual tension and anxiety on the Queen was amazing. For some years before, signs of returning vitality and rejuvenescence had been visible, but this perpetual strain with its constant calls on her judgment was precisely the tonic she needed. Hitherto she had wailed and protested at the cruel way in which she was overworked, at the callousness of those who teased and tormented her to make exertions of which she was incapable: she had been full of self-pity for the lonely lot of the "poor Queen," but now there was an end of that. Instead of insisting on remaining at Osborne or fleeing to Balmoral to the great inconvenience of her Ministers, she positively offered to leave her retreats for Windsor, and instead of having to be urged by her Ministers to a greater activity it was she who spurred and hustled them. No doubt the fact that she was working with a Prime Minister who was congenial to her both personally and politically, instead of one whose policy she detested, and whose exhortations only made her resistance more stubborn, helped in this restoration; for now, as Disraeli had once put it, she gave her Prime Minister inspiration, and he gave her devotion.

Physically as well all her energy was pouring back: she reviewed troops, she went on board her ships, and found she had not forgotten her sea-legs: she went to see a game of La Crosse; she received that queer man Mr. Richard Wagner, who wrote such extraordinary music – surely

Victorian 'scrap' of the Queen with her ministers,
Disraeli and Lord Salisbury.

Germany was a little mad about him – she had an impromptu dance at Osborne, "and I danced a Quadrille and a valse (which I had not done for eighteen years) with dear Arthur, who valses extremely well, and I found I could do it, as well as ever!": and up at Balmoral the "Great Expeditions" were renewed. Perhaps her energies had been unimpaired throughout the long twilight of her seclusion, but they had been devoted to guarding it, and to resisting enjoyment. Now, spontaneously, she was enjoying again, and never surely in the history of nervous disorders was there a more triumphant and lasting recovery; as each New Year came round, instead of looking backwards with regrets for vanished happiness, she prayed for renewed strength to improve, and do her duty and fulfil her arduous task.

All her sagacity and shrewdness, which had been overshadowed by her melancholy, beamed out again. The Crown Princess of Prussia, for ever veering round like a weathercock, always clever and never wise, wrote her a letter of advice, saying that all lovers of England were so anxious that she should take this opportunity, when Turkey's troubles were thick on her, of annexing Egypt. Bismarck, she told her mother, was convinced

'Scrap': Victoria supported by two of her sons.

that England "ought" to do so for he considered that "a strong England" would be of great use in Europe. Was it not a cause for rejoicing that Bismarck should feel like that? In answer the poor lady got a reply of withering perspicacity:

"I will now answer your letter of the 11th relative to Egypt, the proposal about which *coming from you* has indeed surprised me very much, and seems to me Bismarck's view. Neither *Turkey* or *Egypt* have done *anything* to offend *us*. Why should *we* make a *wanton* aggression, such as the taking of Egypt would be? It is not *our* custom to *annex countries* (as it is in *some others*) unless we are obliged and forced to do so, as in the case of the Transvaal Republic: Prince Bismarck would probably like us to seize Egypt, as it would be giving a great slap in the face of France, and be taking a mean advantage of her inability to protest.

It would be a *most* greedy action. I own I *can't* for a moment understand *your* suggesting it. What we *intend* to do we *shall* do without Prince Bismarck's permission . . . How can *we* protest against *Russia's* doings if *we* do the *same* ourselves?"

Another sign of her emergence from the twilight was her recognition of the Prince of Wales's abilities, because it testified to the liberation of her mind from its pathetic dependence on the Prince Consort's infallibility. He had pronounced his son stupid because he had no love of books, and frivolous because he was sociable. It was a mistake that might easily be made by an extremely conscientious man whose valuation of the gifts of others was based on their coincidence with his own, and the Queen, hitherto accepting him as incarnate wisdom, was now at last slipping off that shackling conviction. As for herself, though her devotion to the Prince Consort's memory was as lovingly steadfast as ever, she no longer felt the helplessness with which the deprivation of his counsels had once crushed her. She trusted again to the conclusions of her own extremely shrewd mind, without miserably groping for guidance from her knowledge of what he had laid down. Though her mind had grown in no way more subtle, experience had greatly enriched and matured it, giving her vast stores of sound knowledge on which swiftly and instinctively to base her decisions. In this sense the Albertian age had passed, and the Victorian age had begun.

Early in 1880 Lord Beaconsfield's Government was defeated and yet again Gladstone became Prime Minister. Within six months the Queen was writing to Lord Beaconsfield: "I *never* write except on formal *official* matters to the Prime Minister . . . I look always to *you* for ultimate help." Most acutely did she feel the loss of friendly and confident relations with him and the difficulty of working with a man whom politically she thoroughly mistrusted.

But the new year was full of trouble for her both personally and politically. There was Lord Beaconsfield's death in April, and in both respects that was a cruel stroke. Since the death of the Prince Consort twenty years before there had been no-one on whose political wisdom she more relied, and none with whom she had been on terms of such personal affection. For the moment all dissensions were stilled, and she and her Prime Minister shook hands over the memory of "her dear great friend."

The antagonisms between these two incompatible natures were resumed. There had been a serious disaster to British arms in South Africa at Majuba Hill early in 1881. General Roberts was sent out, but before he got there peace had been arranged and the Boers regained their independence under British suzerainty. To the Queen's imperialistic sense this was

The populace of Windsor abuse Roderick Maclean as he
is driven to the police station after his attempt on the
Queen's life.

monstrous and most damaging to the prestige of the Empire, and she thoroughly distrusted, as it proved with reason, such misplaced magnanimity. In the autumn trouble began in Egypt, and Bismarck saw the fruit of his suggestion that England should take Egypt pleasantly ripening on its own account. Arabi, the Khedive Tewfik's Minister of War, raised a military revolt against the Dual Control of England and France, and in the summer of 1882 a serious riot in Alexandria occurred: some fifty French and English subjects were killed, and Arabi began to construct earthworks to defend the town against the English and French fleets. A bombardment ensued, but the French Government ordered their fleet to take no part in it, and the English acted alone in that and in the subsequent defeat of Arabi at Tel-el-Kebir. Twelve thousand British troops remained in the country, and though France had refused to take any hand in putting the rebellion down, she looked with strong suspicion on the action of the English and on this temporary occupation, which somehow suggested an idea of permanence.

These years were chequered with personal troubles and bereavement as well as with anxieties for the Empire. In 1882, just as she had got into her carriage at Windsor station, a man called Roderick Maclean fired at her with a revolver. This was the seventh outrage of the sort during her reign, but this time the pistol was loaded and it was a real attempt on her life. Maclean was tried for high treason, and to the Queen's strong disapproval was pronounced not guilty but insane. Next year John Brown died. Since the Prince Consort's death he had been her constant attendant wherever she was; he was often peremptory and rude to her, he was far too fond of whisky, he was intolerable to visitors at Balmoral and Osborne, patting Ministers on the back and being odiously familiar to the family, but she had got to depend on him and his close, personal attendance in a manner both touching and ludicrous. As a youth he had been the Prince Consort's gillie, and, in that long morbid twilight in which she had wrapped herself after the Prince's death, it was not unnatural that he should have become to her a link with her husband and those happy holidays in the Highlands, and the "Great Expeditions." Some sentimental supposition of the sort may explain her devotion to him and the unresented liberties he took with her, which she would not have tolerated from any other living being. Her grief at his loss was very sincere, it was the loss of another real friend, and there was inserted in the Court Circular a panegyric on her faithful servant to whom she dedicated her new volume of extracts from her Journal about her life in the Highlands. She put up a statue to him on an eminence at Balmoral; her Laureate, at her request wrote the dedicatory inscription:

> "Friend more than Servant, loyal, truthful, brave
> Self less than duty even to the grave."

In autumn 1883 the prophet Mahdi raised a rebellion in the Sudan. There were many Egyptian garrisons scattered over the country and,

Four generations in 1886: Queen Victoria, smiling,
beside her daughter Beatrice, Princess Henry of
Battenberg (STANDING); her grand-daughter, Victoria,
Princess Louis of Battenberg, who holds her daughter,
Princess Alice of Battenberg, on her lap.

with the Queen's approval, General Gordon, who knew the native races better than any European, was sent out to evacuate these posts. But she herself was indecisive: she could not clearly determine what she wanted done, writing to Sir Evelyn Wood one day that Gordon ought to have been sent long ago, and a week afterwards to Gladstone "trembling for his safety." An atmosphere of nerves was abroad, nobody could make up his mind. In Cairo the Consul General Sir Evelyn Baring was very doubtful as to the expediency of attempting the evacuation, and first he considered Gordon quite unfit for it, and then that he was the best man to employ provided that his programme was clearly laid down for him. Gordon himself was equally indeterminate: when he arrived at Khartoum he was confident that the job would be finished in six months, and then he took another line, and urged the powers at Cairo to send him British or Indian troops and he would "smash the Mahdi." But this was not the mission with which he had been entrusted.

By April 1884 the Mahdi's forces were investing Khartoum, and some expedition must clearly be sent for its relief. Interminable delays followed, but these were not wholly the fault of the Government but of the military authorities who could not agree upon the route it should take. Eventually it was decided to proceed *via* the Nile, and in August Lord Wolseley was sent out in command: in January 1885 a successful action at Abu Klea opened the way to Khartoum. But these procrastinations, for which the Queen blamed her Government, and her own presage of disaster had got cruelly on her nerves.

Her forebodings were only too well founded. On January 20, General Gordon sent down four steamers from Khartoum to meet the expedition, and Sir Charles Wilson, in charge of the advance guard, fought his way up the Nile with two of them. When they came within sight of Khartoum, the Egyptian flag no longer flew on Government House. Khartoum had fallen, and General Gordon had been killed. Personally she never forgave Mr. Gladstone for the fatal delay for which she chose to consider the Cabinet wholly responsible.

In the summer of 1885 there occurred an event which brought to the Queen a greater brightness and happiness in her domestic life than had been hers since the death of the Prince Consort twenty-four years ago, namely the marriage of her youngest daughter Princess Beatrice to Prince Henry of Battenberg. He was the youngest of the three morganatic sons of Prince Alexander of Hesse, uncle of the Grand Duke of Hesse who had married Princess Alice. His eldest brother Prince Louis had married the Queen's granddaughter Princess Victoria of Hesse and was now a Commander in the British Navy, while the second, Prince Alexander, was reigning Prince of Bulgaria. It was settled that Prince Henry and his wife should live with the Queen, whether at Osborne or Windsor or Balmoral, and instantly he made a sparkle and a gaiety in her home which had not been there through all the years of her widowhood. The Queen was devoted to him and he to her and he became the ideal son-in-law no less than the ideal husband. She was genuinely fond of music and he got Tosti to arrange musical evenings for her: she immensely enjoyed a play, and London companies came down to act at Windsor. Day after day people of note, such as the Queen would be interested to see, dined and slept there. As the years passed, grandchildren increased and there were tableaux the rehearsals of which she punctiliously attended and expressed the utmost astonishment and admiration of their performance. Rejuvenance of energy had already come to her: now there was added to that an intimate tenderness and indulgence. Prince Henry was infinitely thoughtful for her, and how she loved the fun and the enjoyment of this altered atmosphere!

In 1886 there was further cause for rejoicing when Gladstone was defeated over the issue of Home Rule and Lord Salisbury became Prime Minister.

Jubilee wallpaper produced in 1887: the Queen and
Empress surrounded by vignettes of her colonies in four
continents.

ILLUSTRATED LONDON NEWS picture of Queen
Victoria's visit to the 'Wild West' show of the Great
American Exhibition.

XII · GOLDEN JUBILEE

THE QUEEN WAS getting on for seventy; only the quite elderly could remember the days when she had not been Queen of England, she was the mother of many children, and had suffered many bereavements. Even her long seclusion, so highly unpopular at the time, intensified the national feeling about her, for during it she had become something of a legend: and now at her approaching Jubilee all these sentiments were focussed into a manifestation of personal loyalty and affection, which for the remainder of her life was to shine steadfast without eclipse. No King could ever have attained such a position, the fact that she was a woman was an essential part of it.

The Queen's public appearances in 1886 had not been more numerous than usual, but in the spring of 1887 she spent ten days at Buckingham Palace, a longer sojourn than she had ever made there since the death of the Prince Consort in 1861. The chief ceremony of the Jubilee was to be the Service in Westminster Abbey on June 21, and she felt it would be an ordeal, for emotional memories would be thick about her, and the service must not be too long "for the weather," she wrote to the Archbishop, "will probably be hot, and the Queen feels faint if it is hot." She had not entered the Abbey for any function since, as a girl of nineteen, she had been crowned there forty-nine years ago, and now she went to see the preparations for her Jubilee. There was the Coronation Chair set over the stone from Scone, just where she had sat before, and with her Lord Chamberlain and "the amiable little Dean Bradley" and officers of the Board of Works, she discussed all the arrangements and she hoped there would be "room for everybody and everything." Indeed the vigour of her young days had returned, for before she went back to Windsor that night she drove to Earl's Court, and saw Buffalo Bill's "Wild West" and found it "very extraordinary and interesting." Three days later, up she came from Windsor again and drove in semi-state from Paddington through the City to Mile End where she opened the People's Palace. It was a progress of fifteen miles through crowded streets and, considering the mass of Socialists and "low bad Irish who abound in London," two or three of whom, she thought, went from place to place, in order to raise faint booings as she passed, her reception was most enthusiastic. She stopped at the Albert Docks, she had tea at the Mansion House, and two days afterwards received six addresses at Windsor, and the Maharajah of Kuch Behar and his wife came to stay for two nights. Any one of these engagements a few years before would have entailed bitter protests and long periods of rest before and after. She came up to London the morning before the Jubilee day. She greeted twenty Royal guests in the Picture Gallery and lunched with them. She gave many audiences afterwards, and more Royal guests arrived, and there was an immense dinner in the evening.

The Queen had quite made up her mind as to the personal appearance she would present on that day. Attempts had been made to induce her to wear robes of state: the last to try had been the Princess of Wales, who came out baffled from the Presence saying she had never received such a snub in her life. For she would have neither crown nor sceptre nor robes, nor would she drive in the monstrous gold coach, the swaying of which always made her feel rather unwell, but in a landau, alone on the back seat, with the Crown Princess of Germany and the Princess of Wales opposite her. There was a separate procession of Sovereigns; a cavalcade

Jubilee souvenir: a genealogical tree of Victoria and
Albert.

the ROYAL OAK

VICTORIA REGINA 1837-1887.

of relations, three sons, five sons-in-law, nine grandsons and grandsons-in-law preceded her on horseback, Princesses followed in carriages. The glittering lines passed up the nave of the Abbey, and the central figure to whom all had come to do honour was a little old lady, walking slowly and leaning on a stick, dressed in black satin with a white front and a white bonnet with a black velvet band, and she had come to church to thank God for all His mercies to her and to the Realm over which fifty years ago He had called her to rule. Her eyes were dim when the *Te Deum* was sung, for Albert had composed it, and in the anthem there was incorporated his chorale "Gotha" which he had played to Mendelssohn on his new organ at Buckingham Palace nearly fifty years ago. Every moment and incident of this day she recorded in her Journal: home at a quarter to three, and lunch with all her Royal guests at four, and the presents she was given – the Queen of Hawaii's gift was a sort of picture: a wreath of rare feathers strangely arranged round her monogram also in feathers, stuck on to a black ground and framed – a great dinner, with Highland pipers playing and healths drunk, a reception of the Corps Diplomatique, and once more, as forty-nine years ago, she looked out at the illuminations in the Park.

Next day there were more deputations and more presents and before leaving London she attended a vast gathering of school-children in Hyde Park. She drove from Slough to Windsor and received two addresses at Eton, and gave a large family dinner. Before it was over the torchlight procession of Eton boys had arrived, and she hurried down to the Quadrangle and thanked them in as loud a voice as she could, so that they should all hear her. The town was illuminated, but she was too tired to go out again.

At length there was a little quiet for her at Osborne, and with her dogs round her she breakfasted on the lawn under a great green umbrella, and when breakfast was done, she attended to the contents of the despatch-boxes from Governmental Departments, and when that was done one of her Indian attendants Munshi Abdul Karim came to give her a lesson in Hindustani: to know a little of the language brought her into better contact with the people of her Empire. When next she had Indian princes to receive she ventured on a sentence in their native tongue to greet them, and presented them to Princess Henry of Battenberg in the same language. Henceforth, and till the end of her life, she was waited on by Indian servants: one pushed her wheeled chair down the corridors at Windsor, and stood behind her at lunch and dinner, and whether at Balmoral or Windsor or Osborne, Munshi Abdul Karim gave her daily lessons in Hindustani. At Windsor he lived in Frogmore Cottage. Other Indian attendants occupied King John's Tower, where they were allowed to kill and cook fowls with their native rites. A smell of blood and onions and curry reminded them of home.

When Crown Prince Frederick of Prussia succeeded his father he was a dying man; cancer of the throat had been diagnosed. In 1888 the Queen determined to go to Berlin to see her beloved son-in-law once more and also by her presence to show her sympathy with her daughter, although relations between Prussia and England were strained and Lord Salisbury was against the visit.

The Emperor of Austria, with her permission, travelled seventy miles to have lunch with her at Innsbruck, and though she had a bad sick headache, they had a most satisfactory conversation and an affectionate parting. In the late afternoon the Queen Mother of Bavaria, and the Prince Regent met her at Munich with a bouquet of roses and a book in which she signed her name. She admired the scenery and the lovely *Alpenglühen* on the mountains, and then she worked till bedtime, travelled through the night, and arrived at Charlottenburg early next morning. Her amazing memory and fluent pen noted and recorded everything: the huge sentries with drawn swords for the reception of a Sovereign: her rooms once occupied by Frederick the Great, and never used since: her tidying of herself: a visit to Fritz in bed: breakfast with Vicky and her girls: an interview with Sir Morell Mackenzie: a very sad talk with poor Vicky: a drive into Berlin in the afternoon: a visit to the widowed Empress Augusta "quite crumpled up and deathly pale," a visit to Vicky's palace in Berlin, and a large family dinner of twenty-five persons. All this was on the day succeeding a journey of twenty-four hours with a night in the train: could it indeed be the same woman who, nearly twenty years younger, must rest at Osborne for ten days after opening Parliament?

Bismark had asked for an interview: she was quite willing to see "the unbearable tyrant," and fixed an hour on the following morning. He nervously enquired of her Secretary in what part of the room she would be? He could make fun of her when she was safe in England, but when she was just the other side of the door, waiting for him, the fun evaporated, and left a thick sediment of terror. But he got in somehow, and she asked him to sit down, and she found him "amiable and gentle." They spoke of the international situation in Europe, of the tragic reason for her visit; he agreed with her about the cruel position of the Empress Frederick and about the Crown Prince William's inexperience.

The Emperor Frederick died on June 15, 1888 within a year of his splendid appearance at the Queen's Jubilee. Her grief at his loss, as for a son of her own, and her sympathy with her daughter were profound and poignant, and there was also alarm for the future. For thirty years he and his wife had prepared themselves for this reign which had proved to be three months of dying, and Germany, instead of being guided by a wise and moderate and liberal-minded Emperor was now in the hands of a Chancellor, ruthless and unscrupulous, and of a young man rash and inexperienced, and grotesquely but perilously intoxicated with the sense of his own power.

It had been a sad year and a disturbing one. William was rude and huffy, and the Queen was very much upset about the series of murders by Jack the Ripper in East London, and she thought they should employ more detectives; and Abdul Karim went on leave to India and she had to study Hindustani alone; and the President of the United States had dismissed the British Ambassador. A bright spot was that her relations with the Prince of Wales had been extremely good: again and again she noted in her Journal what "a dutiful and affectionate son he was to her." But at Osborne on the last day of the year, no-one felt like sitting up to see in the New Year 1889.

The Queen stayed at Sandringham next spring: she always took a child-like delight in a play, and the Prince had got Henry Irving and his company to act "The Bells." She was thrilled. Then there were domestic affairs to discuss: the Prince's eldest daughter, Princess Louise, was to marry the Earl (created Duke) of Fife, and his elder son Prince Albert

The Prince of Wales with his wife and children at
Marlborough House in 1889: (LEFT TO RIGHT) Duke of
Clarence, Princess Maud, Princess of Wales, Princess
Louise, (SITTING) Prince George and Princess Victoria.

Victor was now twenty-five, and the delicate question of further grants
for the maintenance of the Royal House had to be reopened. Gladstone,
who had invariably been a staunch supporter of these grants, promised
his support again, but there was a good deal of Radical opposition. A
Committee of all parties in the House was appointed to consider the
matter, and though the Queen was "quite horrified to see the name of
that horrible lying Labouchere, and of that rebel Parnell" among its
members, the "Prince of Wales's Children Bill" passed by a sound
majority, in spite of Labouchere's assurances to the House that the
Queen was rich enough to provide amply for all her grandchildren. The

Bill gave the Prince an additional £36,000 a year out of which he was at his own discretion to make provision for his children, and was really a very handsome endowment. He was extremely grateful to Gladstone for his support, but it is to be feared that the Queen had no such feelings.

Her seventieth birthday came round; she felt very far removed from those birthdays of her married life, but though the snows were white on

A PUNCH cartoon of 1890 illustrating Europe's
nervousness at the Kaiser's antics.

her own head, and so much belonged to the past, it was now not the past in which her mind dwelt, but the future, and it was full of spring flowers and young growth. The Battenberg children, whom she adored, came to see her that day before she was up, and they sat on her bed, and gave her their presents, and wished her "Many happy returns, Gangan." They had lately had a new brother, but they were not pleased with him, and said "Won't kiss that!" She saw the Trooping of the Colours for the first time in her life, and telegrams and letters poured in on her in such numbers that she had not time even to read them all that day. She was very lame, and had a great deal of pain, but physical discomfort and nerves generally no longer worried her, and she went up to London for a garden-party at Marlborough House, and was wheeled about in her bath-chair. There was a very enterprising young lady among Bertie's guests, and the Queen summoned her ladies to form a body-guard, "because," she said, "I see Mrs. — coming, and I know she will try to kiss me . . ." Next day she received the Shah of Persia at Windsor, and Abdul Karim was back from India, and the Hindustani lessons could be resumed again under his tuition. Jean and Edouard de Reszke and Madame Albani came down to sing to her; they were wonderful, and Jean reminded her of the inimitable Mario. Then down she went to Osborne, and the Family collected in force, and in some anxiety, for the coming of William.

Bygones were bygones, and almost feverish symptoms of family affection took their place. The Prince of Wales went out in the *Osborne* to meet the Imperial yacht *Hohenzollern*, and they steamed side by side through the great avenue of British ships assembled for the Naval Review. The Kaiser was in the uniform of Nelson, which he said made him quite giddy, and in order to show that Germany also could do something on the sea, he had no less than twelve German ships of war as his escort. He was most respectful and affectionate to his grandmother; he breakfasted with her every morning and dined on five nights out of the six evenings of his visit, and they buried the past under a shower of distinctions. He conferred on her the office of Colonel-in-Chief of the Garde-Dragoner, and she duly wore the regimental colours on her shoulder, and he gave her a marble bust of himself in a helmet, and for Prince George of Wales there was the order of the Black Eagle. In turn the Queen invested his brother Prince Henry with the Garter, and gave Count Herbert Bismarck "a beautiful box" and sent his father a copy of Von Angeli's portrait of herself. But the bulk of entertainment fell on the Prince: he took his nephew to dine at the Royal Yacht Club and made him a member (which he lived bitterly to regret): he went daily with him to the regatta: he escorted him on a prolonged inspection of the British fleet, and listened to the Kaiser instructing Captains and Admirals about naval guns. That seemed to have finished him off: he could stand no more, and a bad knee prevented him from accompanying the Kaiser to a military review at Aldershot.

Prince Albert Victor (Eddy), Duke of Clarence, in 1891,
the year of his engagement to Princess Mary and of his
death.

The Queen working at Frogmore in 1893.

XIII · A Magnificent Matriarchate

THE QUEEN'S VIGOUR and enterprise seemed to increase with years. This spring she had been to Biarritz and crossed the frontier into Spain to see the Queen Regent: never before had an English Sovereign set foot on Spanish soil. Then, after William's exhausting visit was over, instead of going straight up to Balmoral for prolonged repose, she went to North Wales and spent four days there in a house lent her near Lake Bala. She took the train to Llangollen (where, she remembered, nearly sixty years ago she had stayed for a night in an inn with her mother on one of those summer tours), and drove to the house of Sir Theodore Martin. It was the anniversary of the Prince Consort's birthday, and Sir Theodore showed her the table at which he had written that monumental "Life" in five volumes. A Welsh choir sang Welsh songs to her, and, just as she had spoken a sentence or two of Hindustani to a Maharanee, now with child-like pleasure she learned up a few words of Welsh, and fired them off at a deputation which had presented her with a walking-stick. The Prince of Wales and his family, she thought, must really come to his principality; it was only five hours from London, and the Princess had

139

never been here at all, and these warm-hearted people felt that he neglected them. Hawarden was not far-off, and Mr. and Mrs. Gladstone had received a terse telegram of congratulation on their Golden Wedding Day a few weeks before, but Mrs. Gladstone's suggestion that the Queen should visit them at their home was not taken up. Her Secretary wrote to say how touched she was, and "how eagerly she had considered the possibility." But her time was too much occupied, and it could not be managed.

In England the spirit of Imperialism continued mightily to flourish, and the Queen to expand with it. Cecil Rhodes, now Prime Minister of Cape Colony, came to England in the early spring of 1891, and, no doubt at Lord Salisbury's suggestion, was bidden to dine at Windsor. The Queen was much impressed by him: he was tremendously strong, absolutely anti-Republican, and he held the very agreeable conviction that England alone out of all the nations of the world knew how to colonize (poor Willie, who just now was very great on German colonizing!). And he had big ideas, ideas after her own heart, for he hoped to see the English rule extend from the Cape to Egypt.

She was enjoying life: she prayed that she might have some years more of it yet; her Houses of Parliament under the present Government were working smoothly: "no bad language," she noted, "and excellent majorities." The Waterloo Gallery was used again for the performance of plays: Mr D'Oyley Carte's Company gave *The Gondoliers* for her, and Mr Hare played *A Pair of Spectacles* and *A Quiet Rubber*.

In June this year (1891) there was the libel action in connection with the baccarat scandal at Tranby Croft, over which the English and indeed the Continental press made such a terrific and wholly disproportionate outcry. It was not a pleasant business for a son of hers to be mixed up in, and the publicity of the witness-box was disagreeable. The Queen was much vexed over this horrid affair, and felt herself obliged to tell him what she thought about it. In fact he got a good scolding and then no more was heard about it, and before long her Journal again recorded what a dear and affectionate son he was to her.

The Princess of Wales had been passing through a rather trying time, and she left England with her two younger daughters in the autumn of 1891 with the intention of spending some months abroad, first at Copenhagen and then with the new Tsar and Tsarina, her sister, in the Crimea. But she had to hurry home for her second son Prince George fell ill of typhoid fever. Those of Coburg blood were curiously susceptible to it: the Queen had had it as a child, the Prince Consort had died of it, the Prince of Wales and the Duke of Edinburgh had both nearly died of it, and Prince Albert Victor, Duke of Clarence, had had it. Prince George got over it well, and while he was convalescing his elder brother became engaged to Princess Victoria Mary of Teck. The Queen thoroughly approved, for Prince Eddy was nearly twenty-eight, and it was high time he married, and she had a great affection for the young lady both for her own sake and because she was the daughter of her best-beloved of cousins, Princess Mary, Duchess of Teck. Perhaps there was a faint memory of the baccarat case and other recent domestic disturbances in her mind when she wrote to the Archbishop of Canterbury saying that the Princess was very charming "with much sense and amiability, and very *un*frivolous, so that I have every hope that the young couple will set an example of a steady quiet life, which, alas, is not the fashion in these days." But grievous tragedy followed. When the Prince was down at Sandringham for the celebration of his birthday on January 9, 1892, he caught a bad cold; it proved to be influenza and he died of pneumonia five days afterwards.

The Queen felt his death very deeply, and only two months later her son-in-law the Grand Duke Louis of Hesse-Darmstadt died also. She went to Hyères in the spring, and came back through Darmstadt to see her orphaned grandchildren: a sad visit, full of memories. But once again that indomitable vitality asserted itself, and her letters dealt fervently with a sheaf of miscellaneous topics. The new coinage would not do at all: her crown was badly put on and her nose was too pointed. Mr Chamberlain was very sound in his views about Egypt. The telegraphic and telephonic communications between light-houses and coast-guard stations must be improved. The "Access to Mountains Bill" if passed in its present form would completely ruin the privacy of the Highlands. There ought to be a closed time of six weeks during which all tourists should be excluded from deer forests . . . Yes: she agreed with Lord Salisbury that it would be terrible if her cousin Prince Ferdinand of

Bulgaria were murdered or driven from his country, and if it would have a good effect she would let him come and stay with her at Balmoral . . . But No! She would not invite William to Osborne this year. If he wished (as he did) to come in his yacht for the Cowes Regatta he must stay on board, and it would be as well if her Ambassador at Berlin "could hint that these regular annual visits are not quite desirable." A great range of topics, with her mind emphatically made up about each.

But the General Election was approaching and the Queen shared her Ministers' fears about the result. The idea of Gladstone being Prime Minister again was a nightmare, and Lord Salisbury's opinion that his passions had become more imperious while he had outlived his judgment, was not reassuring. But whether or no Mr. Gladstone had outlived his judgment, he had certainly not outlived his vigour or his prestige. The Election went against the Government and Gladstonians and Irish Home Rulers combined formed a majority of 355 to 315. The Queen expressed her feelings to Lord Lansdowne on the sad necessity of asking Mr. Gladstone to form a Ministry with unusual clarity: "The danger to the Country, to Europe, to her vast Empire which is involved in having all these great interests entrusted to the shaking hand of an old, wild and incomprehensible man of $82\frac{1}{2}$ is very great!"

So once more the deplorable association between these magnificent and incompatible personages was renewed.

When the Queen's seventy-fourth "poor old birthday," as she henceforth termed it, came round, it was a very happy one, in spite of these political tempests, and she wished she was ten years younger. There were grandchildren with her who acted tableaux for her, and that of "Grandmamma's Birthday" almost moved her to tears. A domestic event had happened which gave her very great and personal pleasure, and in which she had had a considerable hand: Prince George of Wales, now Duke of York, was betrothed to Princess Mary of Teck, whose engagement to his elder brother had been so tragically terminated a little more than a year ago. The Queen came up to London for the ceremony in July, and on the day before attended a gigantic garden party at Marlborough House, recking nothing of the terrific heat, and brought herself to say a cordial word or two to Mrs Gladstone's husband. There was a great family

The wedding group of Prince George and Princess Mary.

dinner – she now enjoyed such functions very much – and the King and
Queen of Denmark, grand-parents of the bridegroom, were there and the
Tsarevitch who was so like the bridegroom that people mistook one for
the other. Next day was the wedding, and she drove in the new State
coach with glass sides up Constitution Hill and along Piccadilly and
down St James's Street to the Chapel Royal. By some mistake in the
timing of the processions she got there first, and much appreciated the
unusual experience of being kept waiting, because she saw the others
arrive. Over fifty-three years ago – how vivid and far away were those
days – Albert and she had been made man and wife on that self-same
spot, and thirty-five years ago her beloved Vicky had stood there. But
now, as an old woman, she was living for the future, full of vivid hopes

and fears, whereas thirty years ago she was mourning for the past.

In September the long looked-for moment came, and the Lords threw out her Prime Minister's Home Rule Bill by the immense majority of 419 against 41: for the rest of the Queen's reign that spectre was laid.

For Gladstone the end had come. In 1894 he wrote to the Queen that he proposed to resign office on grounds of physical disability, and then tendered his resignation in person. He was very old, she recorded, and very deaf, and he said his eyes were getting rapidly worse. She asked him to sit down, and said "she was sorry for the cause of his resignation," which was sufficiently explicit. There were a few words about honours, some neutral topics, and the audience was over. But how bitterly he must have felt the rancour of her frigidity may be gathered from what happened when, three days later, he and Mrs. Gladstone went down to dine and sleep at Windsor before his last Council. The Queen saw Mrs. Gladstone, and recorded the interview: "She was very much upset, poor thing, and asked to be allowed to speak as her husband 'could not speak.' This was to say with many tears, that whatever his errors might have been 'his devotion to your Majesty and the Crown were very great.' She repeated this twice, and begged me to allow her to tell him that I believed it, which I did; for I am convinced it is the case, though at times his actions might have made it difficult to believe." Yet still he could not understand that she meant to part with him without a single word of recognition for over fifty years of strenuous service, and though he had already handed in his notice of resignation, she had not formally accepted it, and he wrote once more. He thanked her for her "condescending kindness" to him. Though at the age of eighty-four he considered that he was mentally capable of continuing his official life, his deafness was a handicap to his work not only in the House, but in the Cabinet, and the cataract from which both his eyes suffered prevented his reading anything with the ease and swiftness necessary for the transaction of his public duties. But she had no intention of giving him another interview, and replied that she had taken leave of him already. He was right, she thought, at his age to seek retirement, and wished him the enjoyment of "peace and quiet, with his excellent and devoted wife, in health and happiness and that his eyesight may improve." That iron vein of sincerity, so admirable a quality in itself, would not allow her to give a word of personal thanks to the man who, she was convinced, had shewn himself again and again a danger to her Empire.

The Queen offered the post of Prime Minister to Lord Rosebery without apparently consulting or notifying Mr Gladstone, and went off to spend a few weeks in Florence. From Florence the Queen went to Coburg in excellent and indefatigable spirits for a Royal gathering so large that even her pen failed at the full enumeration of the "endless numbers" of Princes and Princesses, and after recording a good many, wrote "etc." Two purposes had brought her here; she would be the guest of her son and Albert's reigning in his own principality, and she would attend the marriage of two of her grandchildren, Princess Victoria Melita of Coburg and Ernest Grand Duke of Hesse, son of her daughter Alice. Then, most unexpectedly, her matriarchate was likely to be magnificently enlarged, for the day after his marriage the Tsarevitch Nicholas of Russia and yet another grandchild, Princess Alix of Hesse, sought audience and told her they were engaged. She was "quite thunderstruck"; Russia was so far away, and there was the question of religion, and it seemed impossible that "gentle little simple Alicky should be the great Empress of Russia," but before the year was out the death of Tsar Alexander III had brought that to pass.

Never had the Queen been so full of self-imposed activities: she opened the new Manchester Ship Canal on her way up to Balmoral, she stayed a night at the Pavilion at Aldershot and saw a torchlight procession, Duse played *La Locandiera* for her, and the De Reszkes sang. One thing alone troubled her personally, for her eyesight was beginning to fail. She found the reading of despatches difficult: she complained that her Ministers wrote with pale bad ink and very small handwriting, and Lord Rosebery was the worst offender. Years ago Lord Palmerston had insisted on all drafts and despatches being in a good round distinct hand, and that must be enforced. Probably it was the only doctrine of Lord Palmerston's with which she had ever been in complete agreement.

The Queen and Princess Beatrice at Windsor in 1896.
Detail from memorial card for Queen Victoria.

XIV · REST AT LAST

THE ELECTIONS IN 1895 were fought over Home Rule, Liberal Unionists sided with Conservatives, and a sweeping victory was the result. With Lord Salisbury once more as her Prime Minister, who remained in office till the end of her life, the Queen had a Government with whose policies both at home and abroad she was in complete sympathy.

A new Royal visitor to Windsor in July was Prince Nasrulla Khan, son of the Ameer of Afghanistan, from whom he brought for the Queen a prodigious present of textiles, forty shawls and eight hundred rugs. In turn the Ameer asked, through his son, whom the Queen, he said, had treated like a Mother, if he might have an accredited agent in England, who would let him know from time to time how she was. Then in August the Kaiser paid his promised visit to Cowes. It might be described as "the last and the worst," for he never came again, and was quite odious. It was a very trying time for the Family, and the Kaiser felt deeply hurt at the coldness with which England had met his friendly gestures. He said, on his return to Germany that "he had done with her," and hoped that the Queen would stop the publication of *Punch*.

147

Czar Nicholas II of Russia with the Czarina, Victoria's
grand-daughter, and their baby, the Grand-Duchess
Olga, during their visit to England in 1896.

Like telephone-calls from remote lands came communications on Imperial interests, and to these the Queen always gave her personal attention. Slatin Pasha came to see her, and that was a reminder of the still unvindicated disaster in the Sudan. He had been in captivity since the taking of Khartoum by the Mahdi nearly eleven years ago, and he had grim tales of being shewn Gordon's severed head, and of his own months in chains. Three Christian chiefs from Bechuanaland had come to England, and they said that long expensive journey would be short to them if they might see their mother the Great Queen. So Mr Chamberlain, her new Colonial Secretary, once so rabid a Radical but now so stalwart an Imperialist, brought them down to Osborne. Numerous and sometimes slightly embarrassing had been these Imperial embassies of late years and the Queen received them all.

Twice within the last year she had seen Mr. Rhodes again, and had been more struck with him and his Imperial outlook than ever, and she made him a Privy Councillor.

In 1896 the Queen invited the Tsar and Tsarina with their baby daughter to spend a quiet domestic fortnight with her in September at Balmoral. While the Tsar was here would come the day when she had reigned longer than any English Sovereign. To crown these auspicious events there came the news that Kitchener had taken Dongola in the Sudan, and that the dervishes were in full retreat.

The great family party assembled at the Castle of Albert's creation: four generations of the English House were gathered there, as had never before happened in all its history. Of the first generation was the Queen and her cousin the Duke of Cambridge, of the second the Prince of Wales and other sons and daughters-in-law, of the third the Duke of York and the Empress of all the Russias and other grandchildren, and of the fourth a very small boy, aged two, son of the Duke of York. The Queen found David the most attractive child. The intimacy of the family atmosphere was all that it should be, with drives about the countryside, and planting of commemorative trees and a film of them all moving about on the terrace with the children at play, by that wonderful new cinematograph process, which, like all new appliances of science, gave the Queen a child-like delight — how wonderful, for instance, she had found it to listen to speeches at the Mayoral banquet at Liverpool on the telephone while she dined at home, or to speak to a phonograph cylinder, knowing that King Menelik would hear her gracious message in her own voice out in Abyssinia.

The Queen's Diamond Jubilee was approaching, for on June 20, 1897 she would complete the sixtieth year of her reign, and six months before that date the Kaiser was making enquiries about his coming and asking if he should bring some of his children with him, though it had been already settled (and he knew it) that no reigning monarchs at all were to be invited. The Prince of Wales had dreadful qualms that the Queen might allow him to come, for his mother had put in a word for him, and he wrote in great agitation to the Queen's Secretary, saying that he would try to boss everything and would make endless trouble, and she would certainly regret having asked him. But he was reassured: the Queen said she had not the slightest intention of allowing it; "it would never do for many reasons," among which no doubt a forcible one was that she did not wish her Jubilee to be as full of disagreeable family frictions as those frightful Cowes regattas had been. Besides, this celebration was to be entirely different in character from the Jubilee of 1887, when Kings of foreign lands came with their homage. It was to be a festival of Empire, a great gathering of representatives from the Colonies and Dominions, coming to pay their affectionate respects to their Queen and Mother.

It was "Mother" that she had become in popular sentiment, and even as the policeman outside Buckingham Palace, when asked by a bystander why the flag was flying, replied "Mother's come 'ome," so symbolically to the Empire that was just what she stood for. Ten years ago her Sovereignty and her womanhood had combined to render her to her English people a figure of high romance and sentiment, and now that conception of her, vastly intensified, had spread to the remotest ends of the world. Enormous as had been the expansion of the Empire, the prestige and the Motherhood of the little old lady in black had kept pace with it, and it was this that formed the theme of the coming celebrations.

The Queen was at Balmoral when her "poor old birthday" came round again in May 1897: seventy-eight was a good age, but she prayed for a

The Queen's carriage passing through the City during
her Diamond Jubilee celebrations.

few years more yet. By now the programme for the Jubilee was settled: it had given a good deal of trouble, even though William would not be here to interfere. Her lameness prevented her from taking part in any sort of procession, and the main feature was to be a six mile drive through the streets of London with a pause at the west end of St Paul's Cathedral, for a short service of a *Te Deum* and a few prayers. The suggestion had been put forward that the State landau in which she sat, drawn by the eight cream-coloured horses should proceed up an inclined plane into the Cathedral and stand below the Dome during the service, but on reflection this idea seemed undesirable and was abandoned. The actual anniversary of Accession day occurred on a Sunday, so the celebration was fixed for the Tuesday following, and Sunday was a family gathering at Windsor. The Queen went to service in St George's Chapel in the morning, and sat facing the altar with her children and grandchildren and once more she listened to Albert's *Te Deum*: at the end, as at Westminster Abbey ten years before, they all came up to her and she kissed them. Next day she went up to London, driving from Paddington to Buckingham Palace, noting with joy the beaming faces of the huge crowds and the arch with the motto "Our hearts thy Throne" and the incessant cheering. The Family was in full force and gave her their presents, and among her foreign guests was the Archduke Franz Ferdinand and the Prince of Naples and the Prince of Persia. There was a big dinner that night, and the front of her dress was of gold embroidery worked in India, and afterwards fifteen Colonial Premiers and their wives, and the special envoys from overseas, and the officers of the Indian troops who were to form her escort next day were all presented.

Then came the day itself. There was a slight disappointment in the morning, for she had much wanted to watch from the windows the whole of the colossal procession of troops that was to precede her, but the head of it had already passed. Soon it was time for her to start; the Princess of Wales and Princess Christian sat opposite her in the State landau, but the Empress Frederick could not be with her, for reasons of etiquette, since her rank prevented her from sitting with her back to the horses, and the Queen must be alone to greet her people with no one by her side. As she left the Palace she touched an electric button, and the message she had written was telegraphed to the remotest ends of her

Empire: "From my heart I thank my beloved people. May God bless them . . ." And Mother went for her long drive through the shouting streets.

During this year Kitchener in Egypt had been consolidating the province of Dongola, and preparing for the advance which should wipe out the disaster of 1885 and restore the Sudan to the Khedive. All was ready by the beginning of 1898 and in April the Khalifa's forces were heavily defeated on the river Atbara. Then while he was pushing on towards Khartoum came the death of the man whom the Queen still regarded as having been responsible for the loss of the province and the death of General Gordon, which to her was a blot on the nation's honour. Nothing could efface that conviction or the sense that he had been the enemy of the State, and out of all his sixty years of service she could find nothing for praise except his personal loyalty to her and his readiness to do anything for the Family. She wrote affectionately to Mrs. Gladstone about her loss, but her inflexible sincerity forbade her to give any further word of appreciation, for that would have been a recantation, and false at that. She did not like the Prince of Wales acting as Pall Bearer at the funeral, or his kissing Mrs. Gladstone's hand, which was the most perfect and apt of gestures. But the Queen's last word was "I never liked him, and I will say nothing about him." *Sunt lacrimae rerum.*

The Queen was at Balmoral at the outbreak of the Boer War. Back she went to Windsor, travelling through the night, and arriving there at nine in the morning, and before lunch she drove down to the Cavalry Barracks to inspect the composite regiment of Household troops that were going to the Cape, and spoke to the men and wished them Godspeed, and they cheered her and cheered her and would not stop cheering her, for they like France, identified her with her people. There were countless telegrams from the Cape about the arrival of troops, and daily she interviewed her Ministers and there was never a hint of fatigue.

Then for England came perilous days. On December 10, General Gatacre was defeated at Stormberg, and Lord Methuen at Magersfontein, and before the week was out Sir Redvers Buller, in an attempt to relieve Ladysmith was defeated at Colenso with the loss of ten guns. He telegraphed to the War Office the same night in the most disheartened terms, advising the abandonment of Ladysmith and of the offensive, and the taking up of a defensive position in South Natal. This telegram was sent to the Queen early next morning, and she immediately replied to Lord Lansdowne that it was quite impossible to let Ladysmith go; another attempt to relieve it must be made. The Cabinet had come to the same conclusion and had also decided to send out Lord Roberts to take over the command, with Lord Kitchener as Chief of his Staff.

It was a disastrous week, and she was old and very blind and very lame, but where was the good of being Queen and Mother of her immense Empire, unless she behaved as such? She proceeded to do so.

These set-backs must be retrieved: nothing else mattered, and when Mr Balfour came down to Windsor, and made some melancholy reflection, she pulled him up with the firmest of hands. "Please understand," she said, "that there is no one depressed in my house: we are not interested in the possibilities of defeat: they do not exist." On Boxing Day she gave a tea and an immense Christmas Tree in St George's Hall to the wives and children of Windsor troops. Certainly it had been a sad year, her troops had suffered and she had lost many friends, and she was very anxious about the health of her eldest daughter. But there must be no despondency, and she wrote in her Journal as the final entry for the year:

"In the midst of it all I have, however, to thank God for many mercies and for the splendid unity and loyalty of my Empire. I pray God to bless and preserve all my children, grandchildren, and kind relations and friends, and may there be brighter days in store for us."

Then the tide of war turned, and, during February 1900, Kimberley was relieved, General Cronje was heavily defeated by Lord Roberts at Paardeberg, and, at the end of the month, Ladysmith after a siege of four months was relieved also.

Irish troops had done very gallantly in South Africa, and the Queen was thinking of creating a regiment of Irish Guards, when, by an odd coincidence, the proposal was made to her by Lord Lansdowne, and she sanctioned it at once. As a further recognition all ranks in any Irish regiment were given the distinction of wearing a sprig of shamrock in

Queen Victoria with the wives and children of the
soldiers fighting in the Boer War, 1899.

their head-dress on St Patrick's Day. It was March now, and the time for her spring holiday was near. She wanted change, and, with thoughts of her gallant Irish troops in her mind, she settled to go to Ireland to get it. She had not been there since the Prince Consort's death, and she had never thought to set foot there again, but all the trouble over Home Rule and those Fenian outrages seemed far away, and the Irish, it was said, were very warm-hearted folk, though they had given her a great deal of trouble before now. Her subjects in the remotest of her Colonies had been "so kind to her," and they looked on her with personal love and affection, so perhaps if she went to see her Irish folk they might be kind to her too. But first she must spend a couple of days in London, and she took two long drives through the streets to let her people see that she shared their joys just as she had shared their anxieties. There was no pageant, neither police nor soldiers lined the route; and on one day she drove into the City, and another through streets of the West End, and the enthusiasm, she thought, was greater than at either of her Jubilees. Yet once more she came up from Windsor, and visited the Woolwich Arsenal where 20,000 men worked night and day making munitions, and from there, passing the house where General Gordon had been born, she drove to the Herbert Hospital to see the wounded from South Africa. There were many Irish soldiers among them, and she spoke to them all as she was wheeled through the wards, and everywhere in the streets Mother got the same tumultuous welcome: you could not hear what anyone said for the cheering, and so back to Windsor a little tired.

Early in April she set off for Ireland with her two daughters, Princess Christian and Princess Henry of Battenberg: they all wore bunches of shamrock, and the Queen's bonnet and parasol were embroidered with the same in silver. The long route from Kingstown to Dublin was lined with cheering crowds, and for miles, as in London lately, there was scarcely a soldier or a policeman to guard it, and loyal inscriptions of the friendliest doggerel spanned the road: she could read of herself that:

> "In her a thousand virtues closed
> As Mother Wife and Queen."

She was eighty years old and had come all the way from Windsor, travelling through the night, and had pinned a bunch of shamrock to her jacket and had it embroidered on her bonnet and parasol for all to see, and she was so little, and looked so lonely sitting all by herself on the back seat of her carriage, driving for two hours and a half through the slums of the City and she was so dearly gratified to find that her Irish subjects, as she had hoped, were kind to her, that Nationalists forgot their politics and cheered her from the steps of the City Hall, and Ireland was hers.

It was not much of a holiday. Every morning despatch-boxes and telegrams came in, and sometimes there was bad news from South Africa. Sometimes there was a letter of no moment at all, but how right her Secretary was to show it her. For Private James Humphrey of the Royal Lancaster Regiment had been hit by a Boer bullet, but it had struck the box of the Queen's chocolate which he had on him, and that had saved his life, and Private Humphrey had sent the bullet and the chocolate box to Her Majesty.

There were dinner parties in the evening and music afterwards and evening parties, and wherever she went there was this "wild enthusiasm and affectionate loyalty." Lord Beaconsfield had once told her that during the last two centuries the Sovereign had only spent twenty-one days in Ireland, but when she embarked again on the *Victoria and Albert* she had just doubled that exiguous tale. She slept during most of the crossing, and that was not quite usual, for it was seldom that she slept during the day, and then in her Journal she summed up these busy weeks, peering into the future perhaps as much as recalling the past: "I felt quite sorry that all was over, and that this eventful visit, which caused so much interest and excitement, had, like everything else in this world, come to an end, though I am very tired and long for rest and quiet."

But rest would come soon, and in the interval there was much to do. She went back to Windsor and inspected the officers and men of the *Powerful* and spoke to them, and went in to see them at their dinner. The King and Queen of Sweden and a Prince of Japan came to see her, and Professor Pagenstecher gave her good news about her eyes: there had been no change for the worse in the last three years. She held a Drawing Room at Buckingham Palace, and the crowds that welcomed her were as enthusiastic as ever, but it was sad on her return to Windsor to find her piping bull-finch dead in its cage. There came the best of news from South

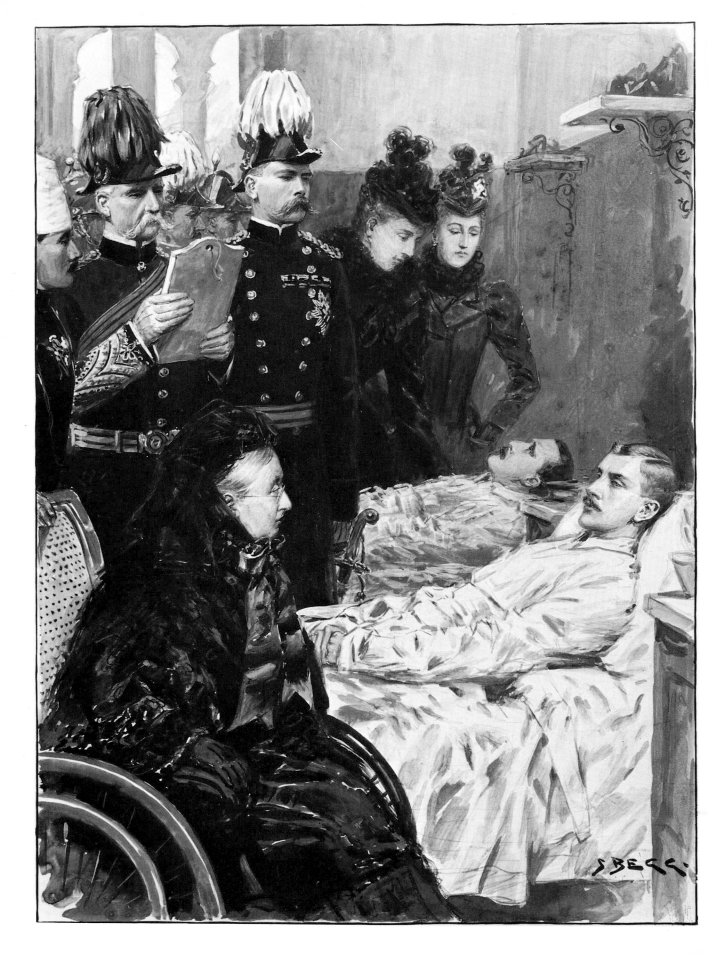